RELEASE

BY
STARR DAILY

Author of *Recovery* and
Love Can Open Prison Doors

RELEASE

STARR DAILY

PUBLISHING

Belleville, Ontario, Canada

All Scripture quotations, unless otherwise specified, are from *The Holy
Bible, King James Version.* Copyright © 1977, 1984, Thomas Nelson
Inc., Publishers.

First printed:
GREAT BRITAIN BY PURNELL AND SONS, LTD.
PAULTON (SOMERSET) AND LONDON

ISBN: 978-1-4600-0323-7
LSI Edition: 978-1-4600-0324-4
E-book ISBN: 978-1-4600-0325-1
(E-book available from the Kindle Store, KOBO and the iBooks Store)

Cataloguing data available from Library and Archives Canada

To order additional copies, visit:
www.essencebookstore.com

Essence Publishing is a Christian Book Publisher dedicated to
furthering the work of Christ through the written word.
For more information, contact:
20 Hanna Court, Belleville, Ontario, Canada K8P 5J2.
Phone: 1-800-238-6376. Fax: (613) 962-3055.
Email: info@essence-publishing.com
Web site: www.essence-publishing.com

TO MY WIFE
in whose brown eyes is
a vision of hope
a light of faith
a glow of love
these three

CONTENTS

FOREWORD

By Professor Glenn Clark

D
ANTE, AFTER HE HAS WANDERED AFAR IN THE FIELDS OF
sorrow and sin, finds himself at last in the dark wood of
despair. Seeing a hill that seems to lead up towards the stars,
he essays to climb it only to find his way blocked by his three sins of
pride, avarice, and lust, which appear before him in the form of a lion,
a wolf, and a leopard. While falling back in despair, there arrives a
messenger "faint voiced through long silence," who tells him he is
Virgil, sent from Hell to guide him to Paradise by the long and cir-
cuitous path of Hell and Purgatory. Then, with Virgil as guide, Dante
is led through the deepest regions of horror and woe until he has seen
all, suffered all, and been purged of all, and is ready at last to enter the
path leading towards Paradise and the whirling stars.

Starr Daily, a Dante of modern times, has gone through the depths
of sin and has suffered the purging fires before he could emerge from his
wood of despair and see the stars. He, too, had a guide through the
Nether Regions, one who had also become "faint voiced through long
silence." The philosophy of Virgil is milk for lambs compared with the
strong meat found in the virile philosophy of the old lifer. Here is a character who is as quickening to new life and as inspiring in moulding men
as the good Bishop in *Les Miserables*. It is certainly a thrilling experience
to sit humbly at the feet of a "lifer" in a penitentiary to get one's greatest
vision of the power of the Love of God that one has ever experienced. Yet
that is exactly what the reading of this book will mean for many people.

In *Love Can Open Prison Doors*, Starr Daily shocked a sleeping
Christendom into a new realization of the tremendous spiritual power

9

lying latent in Jesus' way of life if we only practise it. It is difficult for those raised in sheltered Christian homes to appreciate how difficult it is to help those who come from the deepest valley of sin and suffering, those who have been immersed in the ditches of Malobolg. In this new book, Starr Daily covers the whole gamut of human needs. Out of the deepest pit of sin and the darkest valley of suffering, he comes to tell us of what he has seen and heard, in words that guide us safely over paths which he, himself, has trod. For not only has he travelled the road, but he has recorded his experiences and charted the way.

PROLOGUE

IN ONE MOMENT I WAS A CONFIRMED CRIMINAL. IN THE NEXT I was healed. It was done that quickly. Several have since told me I had come under the grace of God and the action of the Holy Spirit. This I cannot affirm. Nor can I deny it. Frankly I do not know.

I cannot explain the mystery of it. I only know that it was an inner experience of some sort, a huge and different experience. Many men and women have sat down with me to offer their explanations. They've spoken with what seemed authority. Yet in the sober reflective hour that followed I've wondered. I've wondered if such wisdom as they possessed was not as foolishness to God. For though the explanations have been many, they have seldom agreed one with the other. Perhaps they were half-truths, most of them, which made something that was quite simple very complex. I have come to be chary of man's explanations of God's ways. I have seen sagacious explanations fall apart and encounter defeat. I have seen the simple act of embracement by the unskilled and unlettered unify and succeed. I have seen righteous men go to pieces because they lacked the quality of mercy. Rarely, if ever, have I seen a merciful man essay to explain the mystery of God. They seem content to accept and act. It may be that a righteous man plus a merciful man equals one who is pure of heart. Says the sixth Beatitude, such a man shall see God.

Jesus was such a man. He *likened* the Kingdom of God; but He did not explain its mystery. It was given to His disciples to know the mystery of God and the Kingdom. They wrote no books to explain it. They pointed the way. They did not dissect it. "Here is the road," they

11

said. "It's to be travelled: not torn up. It goes to a certain destination. Trust and travel will get you there."

A man with a pick tearing up the road as he goes, pausing long to analyse the stuff out of which the road is made, will progress an inch to the trustful traveller's mile. It is just possible that analysis and explanation of God's Highway offers a dignified excuse for retarding the journey. I've never known a man who possessed the Cross who later explained its mystery. Its critics deny it. Those who look longingly upon it from a distance write books about it, weighty, unreadable books; and deliver addresses, tedious, insufferable addresses.

Always, however, I've been willing to inquire of others more gifted than I in superphysical matters. I have described this transforming experience of mine frankly, and up to the limit of my memory and ability. *I've said that in one tense, dark moment in my life a warm spring of living water welled up in my heart, and a bright unearthly light broke in my head.*

I have said this, also, to a few who likewise had experienced the blessing. These have replied in effect, "Yes, yes, that's it," substituting silence for further explanation.

Apparently those most able to explain these deep, inner experiences of the human soul are those, who, not having had the experience themselves, have been sufficiently detached to study its peculiar action in others, and sufficiently bold to report their findings.

By way of explanation, about the best I can say is that for at least a moment in time I was free of the Time and Space sense; that I knew Reality and knew why I knew it. All of which is no explanation, save for those who are able to say, "Yes, yes, that's it." In this book I shall attempt to describe my experience. I shall not try to explain its mystery. I may state or imply personal conclusions, but not dogmatic ones. I am aware that in describing the experience I shall greatly circumscribe it.

Of an able psychologist I asked, "How do you account for it?" after I had related the occurrence. His reply was prompt and without hesitation, a fact which lessened the power of his authority to speak.

He explained that we have all sorts of psychological abnormalities. We were possessed of many inferior selves, which often found amusement at our expense. They made us walk and talk in our sleep, and to do all manner of odd and freakish things while we were awake, such as using baby talk, mumbling to ourselves, telling lies and fantastical stories, nursing resentments and holding harmful grudges. They caused us to have delusions, exhibit queer mannerisms, airs and pretensions. They caused us to see visions and have hallucinations. They caused us to affect the saint complex, the martyr complex, and to believe in answered prayer when the answer was nothing but the reflex action of auto-suggestion, or self-hypnosis. They caused us to develop religious paranoia, the Hallelujah personality, the divine wedding neuroses, etc., etc., *ad infinitum.*

"Your experience could probably be traced to the prankishness of one of these inferior selves," he finished. "It was like some sort of exalted hallucination."

"Would you say that my ingrained criminal character was reversed by a delusion or hallucination?" I inquired.

He avoided a direct reply to this, and suggested that for some reason there occurred a sudden and radical sublimation of my negative emotions, which acted as a mental gear shifting, and which simply changed my outlook from a lower to a higher level.

The metaphysicians, too, have been vague on the matter, though genuinely sympathetic and interested. Many theologians have expressed doubt. Others have been silent, or have politely changed the subject.

I know little about credal religion. I want to know much. Apart from my experience I have faith. In the experience itself I have fact. Of that I'm convinced. I write here as one jotting down a record of events, a kind of expository narrative concerning an adventure with the teachings of Jesus in prison. It is a first person document all the way. In this fact there is, I hope, no desire to dramatize myself or unwholesomely to exploit a delicate theme. I would not consciously build up sensational

13

effects to enforce a religious argument or to defend a religious view-point. I simply write as one who would report and share an experience, which turned my life upside-down.

Over against my experience lies theology. I must admit that here I am at a loss. For me this would be dangerous ground. At the moment, at least, I dare not trespass too far upon it. The pitfalls are too many for a novice. There are able scholars who are at home in this field of religious controversy. They move with confidence and assurance among the conflicting creeds and waning doctrines, while for me the controversial Christ is little known. Were I to attempt an understanding of this Christ my end would surely be confusion and final sterility. I cannot trust myself, therefore, to venture in a Christian orbit alien to my life-changing experience. Hence if the reader finds the personal pronoun too much in evidence, he will know the reason. An expansive experience in one direction has become my limitation in another. I trust that my good intention may counteract the effect of egotism or a too heavy personal psychology.

If I know little of the theology of Christ, what then do I know of Him as life? I have come to see Him as the WAY of life. To me He is the precept and example of all that can be known here concerning Reality. As the example He is the Divine Love working through the love of law. As the precept He is the Law of Love made manifest.

I see Christ as the Saviour of mankind, individually and collectively, for except by the Law of Love, I can conceive no genuine salvation. Nor can I perceive salvation present in the man while the love of law is absent. I see everything, therefore, which is less than Christ, or less than the precept and example for which He stands, as a compromise with destiny: a way but not *the* WAY of life.

Likewise I perceive Christianity as man's noblest hope for the ultimate establishment of a workable social science on earth. I perceive this because I see in Christianity the noblest possibility for the competitive nature of man and the co-operative nature of woman to come together in Christ and live for the good of all. I perceive in Christianity the noblest hope for a workable natural science. One of America's most distinguished scientists recently remarked to a friend of mine that except for the spiritual application being made of scientific discoveries those discoveries were worse than useless. A broad statement, a sweeping indictment, a powerful challenge; but a little thought will justify it. Science without Christ is insufficient. It cannot time its discoveries, nor can it control them. In the absence of a redeemed humanity and an adequate social science what it uncovers as a blessing becomes likewise a curse. Finally I perceive in Christianity the noblest of all experience, direct and conscious contact with God through the ever present medium of Christ and the action of the Holy Spirit.

In this I am not unmindful of other religions. ("In my Father's house are many mansions.") All are of the same blood, and all are children of the same God. While there are other folds, I only repeat that no religion can aim higher than the Law of Love, nor inspire any loftier sentiment than the love of Law. So far as I know Christ alone of all the great religious leaders advocated an uncompromising "Give yourself." While the others focused attention upon the *self*, as a method for self-improvement and final self-conquest, He focused attention on the Kingdom, and on the forgetting of *self* in the loving service of the neighbour.

Perhaps a secondary difference between the religion of Christ and that of other great religious leaders is to be found in the factor of Grace, which is essentially a Christian tenet, and which belongs to the Christian by virtue of the fact that he recognizes and accepts it as an authoritative gift from the founder of Christianity Himself.

My knowledge of other religious forms precludes the gift of Grace, as I conceive Grace to be. In these other religions there is justice (Karma) and help for those who help themselves. You must reap what you sow. But Christ is not limited to this concept. He breaks through it at will and by special acts of Grace saves those who will not and cannot help themselves. In Him is the hard justice of the righteous man plus the tender love of the merciful man. I shall point out many examples, my own included, in this volume, of men who were saved by Grace in spite of themselves—all testimonies of seemingly unmerited divine mercy. The case of the Apostle Paul is an outstanding historical example of a man who, from a relative point of view, did not merit the Master's mercy, but who received it nevertheless, and with it an unblemished passport to Glory.

If this Grace were not possible I should in all probability be somewhere today festering in a prison cell, instead of sitting here in my study, a comparatively free man, in a position to go and to come at the Master's beck and call.

To me, then, Christ becomes in practice the love of law: in essence the Law of Love. Not *a* way, but *the* WAY! Full of Grace and Mercy and Authority! A Friend and an Intercessor! A warm, colourful personal Friend upon whom we can call! An Advocate who prompts us to act and then responds to our action! A Companion of the road, a Comrade of the quest! One to whom we belong!

I know that so long as I belong to Christ all good belongs to me. I can rest in Him, forcing no issue, allowing what belongs to me to happen at the right time, and in the right place. When I belong to Him the next thing that happens in my life has got to be the best thing and the right thing.

As the love of law Christ can with ease obey even the narrow and unreasonable laws of men. He can show His followers how to do likewise, how to render to Caesar what belongs to Caesar, while in nowise sacrificing the Higher Law in the lesser obedience.

When I read in the Sermon on the Mount that we are to be known by our fruits, I readily conceive this statement to be parabolic, and the term "fruits" to mean actual spiritual experience. Hence what I know myself about religion, about Christ, the Holy Spirit, or about the letter of God's law does not necessarily constitute the fruits of spiritual experience. What I am by virtue of actual experience of religion, or of Christ, or of the Holy Spirit, or of God's word, I conceive to be the meaning of this scripture, and by this *am-ness* or *being-ness* or *is-ness* I am to be known.

It is not what I know of the mystery of the blood of Jesus that determines my authority to speak, but what I am in the embracement of that sacrificial blood. In other words, what I am in actual Christian character. Thus I can measure the extent of my own Christian standing by the recognition of my own limitations, and in that recognition I can avoid the academic Christian's most successful enemy, self-deception. I can say with truth that in those moments when I completely realize that I belong to Christ, I am something. With equal integrity I can say, in the absence of this realization that I am nothing, wholly unworthy, and that were it not for God's love and Grace, I should perish. Such would be the verdict of untempered justice.

It is not what I know of the mystery of baptism, but how deeply I am immersed in the Spirit of Christ, that counts. It is not what I know of the mystery of the Cross, but how willing I am to hang myself upon it and pay its price, that of the *self* for the SELF, the little love for the BIG LOVE.

In other words, during the experimental stages we can learn about many phases of the Truth sought. But not until experiment has been translated into experience, ritual into realization, have we become more than intellectually identified with the Truth.

And when a verse later Jesus suggests that we cannot gather grapes from thorns and figs from thistles, I perceive another parable, which tells me that I cannot go back to the old thorns of crime and thistles of Godlessness and expect to continue to gather the grapes of my present wellbeing. That old life stands for another kind of experiment and experience, which produces after its kind. I must approach LOVE with love and not with reason. "Wherefore by their fruits ye shall know them."

In my beginnings and fumblings with the parabolic teachings of Jesus I ambled along in a sort of studied soberness. The fact is, I have not felt myself fitted for the study of theology, either by intellectual aptitude or temperamental inclination. Consequently I have been more interested in the qualities of Jesus Christ than in the presentation of those qualities. The practice of His states and qualities appeals more to me than the analysis of them. The example applied outweighs the precept studied.

As I see it from this point of vantage, any passage of scripture that builds a wall between a man and Christ as *the* WAY of life is a passage that should be ignored until it comes to light in experience.

There are scores of such wall-building passages in the Bible, one of the greatest of them being the subject of the Virgin Birth. I do not understand this mystery. Whatever it means I accept on faith, and that puts an end to the matter. The subject stops there. I go on. But it is a mystery that has arrested the spiritual unfoldment of millions, who, by momentarily ignoring it, could have gone forward from glory to glory. Until the spiritual key is given this passage must lead to futile argument, with the danger of ending in pessimistic denial, or death, spiritually speaking. It would be more fruitful to pass on quickly to less hypothetical matters, of which the Bible is rich.

Such is my point of view.

CHAPTER 1

A HOUSE THAT CRIME BUILT

IT PARALLELS A STRAIGHT STRETCH OF THE RIVER. BECAUSE OF crime it sprawls there, a grim symbol of social protest against the strong-arm methods of the morally sick. A grey-brown scar on a narrow thrust of tableland, it connects the water with an overshadowing pile of limestone, hard cliffs which have slept for incredible ages waiting to be disturbed by the sullen, unwilling hands of future quarry slaves.

Viewed from across the river this huge stone structure resembles some medieval fortress, forbidding, massive; impregnable with its ramparts and gun-turrets, its watch towers and battlements. But thus viewed from afar there is a certain venturesome fascination about it, a lure to fancy and to the memory of things heard and read, such as remote times and conditions, the heydays of the feudal barons, unscrupulous hirelings and cutthroats, armoured knights and prized ladies, love and hate, light laughter and bitter tears: for losing rivals black dungeons, luxurious suites for the winners, mystery, romance, tragedy—it is all here on the curtain of fancy.

Drawing closer, however, the scene changes. Remote memory gives way to the delights of present observation. For, if it be a summer day, one sees a deep, level, well-kept lawn, dotted with shrubs and blooming flowers. Through this lawn curves a wide, clean walk, which ends at the steps leading into a stately doorway, broad and high and arched. This doorway is the main entrance into the Administration Building, a rather old and unimposing edifice of red brick and dirty grey stone. Out here in front the gardener's art has transformed an unsightly acre into a sweep of lush green loveliness, much as an unsightly character is often transformed by the magic art of the Master's touch. It is upon this beauty that the eye of every prison visitor first falls. And this is good for the visitor whose idea of the prison house has been entirely formed by morbid fiction, and whose idea of a convict has been fashioned out of the stuff from which Big House motion pictures are made.

Just inside the entrance is a huge iron door, which swings ponderously from the hand of a uniformed guard. As a usual thing he is a carefully chosen man. For this particular job a winning smile and a jovial disposition are favourable assets. He is, in fact, quite the equal of any first-rate doorman of any first-rate hotel, minus the latter's passion for tips and eye for quality luggage. The rule here is, "Abandon luggage ye who enter in."

Now that we have passed the winning smile and the ponderous door, we find ourselves in a large, rather austere reception room. The tile floor is highly polished by unrewarded toil. The ceiling is lofty, panelled, dust and cobweb free. The walls are spotless and glisten in their calcimine finish. At the far end of the room is a long table, which is divided in the centre by a screen. On one side of the table may be seen men in the regulation prison grey or blue according to their grade. The other side is reserved for their visiting friends and relatives, and of course their lawyers, who come to give them hope, refer mysteriously to new evidence, and thus earn their fee.

Near the opposite end of the visitors' table is another door, which leads down into the prison proper. It too is manned by a uniformed guard, who may or may not be so genial, for he is closer to the atmosphere of repression and the suffocating reality of prison life.

By now we have a pleasant escort whose speciality is talk. He is a skilled descriptionist. The inner door swings open. Just beyond we pause on the iron platform above the steps, which lead down into the prison yard. From this point we get our first bird's eye view of the inside prison.

We might be looking down a rather drowsy main street. There are no parked cars. What traffic we see consists of a truck or a mule-drawn wagon. There may be a few idlers along the walk, prisoners enjoying the fruits of special privilege. Or a warder or two may be observed loitering near a building. The inevitable convict "runners" are hurrying to and fro with slips of paper in their hands, conveying good news and bad. As we stand here our escort goes into verbal action. He becomes our narrator as well as guide.

"That's an old foundry way down yonder," he says, pointing down the street toward an old dilapidated brick building. "Don't use it for that any more. The fires went out with contract labour in this state. The weak sisters used to die down there. The strong boys went mad. She was purty tough around here in those days. The tasks were hard, the hours long, and food was scant and poor. Old-timers still tell about men ramming their hands in molten ladles of metal, jest to get out of the place. A great change, since then. It's used now for a storage house. Just back of it is where we exercise the old 'stir bugs.' They're the prison cranks."

Here he becomes analytical as well as descriptive.

"They makes little ones out of big ones," he says tritely, and then adds, "If they happen to feel in the mood."

This last implies official indulgence or kindness. Around election day the enemies of the Administration play it up as "coddling." He waits for the information to register on our minds. Then: "But mostly they argue politics and prison history. They all know what's wrong with the world. And you couldn't find one without a plan for its salvation. None of 'em are guilty. They're all victims of circumstances. They know the cause and cure for crime too. Once in a while they knife each other. Or bang a head instead of a rock."

He now becomes a solemn authority and prophet: "They're the old burned out prison lags. Been in most all their lives. They'll end their days in prison. We call 'em stir bugs. They're kind o' weak minded, childish and silly-like. Man's apt to get that way after he's served ten years. It's a kind of harmless insanity. They jest get overfond of prison life and grub. Get so they don't feel at home anywhere else. Some of em have eaten so much prison hash they've turned brown on the outside." Lowering his voice to a confidential tone, he adds, "We've got old warders in here jest about as bad."

He next points out the mess hall and commissary. He directs our gaze to various prison shops, contrasting the old working conditions against the new. He speaks of the hospital building with unveiled pride, referring to it as a modern health plant, and comments lengthily upon its services to the prison body. Pointing to the barber shop he releases an interesting bit of local colour. The barbers used to carry their tools over the prison yard. In the winter time shaving had been a race against freezing lather.

"That's the new laundry right over there," he says. "One of the best money can buy. That fat feller across yonder is our butcher. His shop's in that building he's holding up. In the back of it is our mattress works, ice-plant, tobacco shop and plumbing. The boiler house and power plant is across the alley. That's the brickyard below there. Back over here is the Yard Office. Right behind it, that square dark building, is the solitary, where the boys are punished for misconduct. They call it the 'hole.' They always make the best sound the worst. They call the Deputy Warden *The Man*. He don't mind it. Away over yonder are the rock quarries and play grounds. You can see the rock crusher and dust mill back there to the right. Stone and dust is our business."

With this we follow him down the iron steps and enter one of the long cell houses. Pausing just inside the door we gaze down the lengthy corridor with its glistening flagstones, its high barred windows, its massive, towering cell block, with lane upon lane of barred doors which mark the cells of those who have come to the end, temporarily at least, of their careers in crime. Grouped about our escort we begin our pilgrimage around the giant honeycomb of steel and stone.

"These paddles on the doors are the names and numbers of the men inside," he informs us. We follow him up to one of the doors. Without shame we allow our curious eyes to penetrate the private den of another's shame, perhaps to judge consciously or unconsciously the occupants, or to feel a shudder or a sense of pity; or, if we are big enough, to feel a surge of gratitude for the grace of God which has spared us from prison fare.

The cell is a tiny, crowded niche. Running across the rear is a shelf draped with a piece of stained cheesecloth. The shelf is piled high with plunder, the convict's earthly goods. Below the shelf is a small iron door, like the door of a furnace, fitted to a square hole in the rear wall. We are told that here is where the inmate caches his night bucket.

"They're allowed to decorate their walls with pictures—that is, within reason," our escort tells us.

In the ceiling near the door is an electric light bulb, under which hangs a small mirror. Across the top of the door is stretched a piece of printed percale with a fringe. This substitutes for a scarf. It is a rather pathetic attempt to relieve the drab interior, to cling to the innate response to beauty. On the floor is a painted water bucket. The cell contains a double-decker iron bunk and two stools. Between the bunk and the opposite wall is a narrow passage eight feet long. The stone floor is pitted with measured hollows, worn there by the pacing feet of many convicts, or perhaps by the feet of one convict who thus has worn away the rock along with his life sentence.

We move on. After a while we come to another cell. Here our guide stops with an air of mystery and an attitude that borders well-nigh on reverence. We all feel his mood and become expectant. We wonder why he is pausing here, especially. In fact, this particular cell seems far less attractive than the other one we have just examined. Here we see no extra frills or attempts at finery. Save for a small Hofmann Christ Head the place is entirely barren of pictures and other decorative items. There isn't even the universal cheesecloth shelf cover and percale door scarf. Except for an ancient Bible and a couple of other worn, thin volumes the shelf is bare. The cell, however, is clean, scrupulously clean, and we seem to sense something of the character of the man who occupies it. The paddle on the door, too, seems to hold our attention. It has the appearance of great age. We have to draw close to make out the faded name and number on it.

"He's our senior prisoner, our first man," says the guide, as though he were awed by this fact. "We've got lots of lifers in here. But he's The Lifer." He observes each member in the group, and then adds: "He's been here more years than some of you have been on earth, I reckon. Everybody likes him from the warden down to the lowest stool pigeon. He's always telling jokes and stories. Sort of just makes them up as he goes. Some say that he hides a wise mind behind his yarns. I can't say about that. But every prison has its one personality. He's ours."

"Why is that?" someone asks.

"Well, it ain't all because he's been here so long," our escort replied. "If you were around here a little you'd hear a lot of stories about fellows who have gone out to make good. Some of them have made purty good names for themselves. Desperate criminals have been put in the cell with The Lifer. They've gone in ignorant and bitter. Many of them have come out changed. You could get into trouble mighty easy if you said anything against The Lifer."

Feeling a little awed ourselves we continue our journey around the cell block. Someone suggests that his conception of a convict has been rather vague, a sort of cross between a high class chimpanzee and a low grade moron. Now he is quite surprised to discover that, even in his prison garb, the convict is not so far different from the rest of the human lot. At this our guide and narrator laughs heartily, and then retells an old prison story.

"Well, sir," he begins, "a grand lady came to visit prison one day. She had the same notion you had about prisoners. She thought maybe they might be human. But she didn't know whether they were more animal than man. She was taken to the mess hall at supper time. And you know while she was there she made a great discovery. And, sir, she turned it right loose on an old burglar sitting next to the aisle. 'Why, you even have knives and forks with which to eat, haven't you!' she exclaimed, hardly able to believe her eyes. Out of the corner of his mouth the old burglar replied: 'Oh, yes, madam! Why, we even have teeth.' I guess a lot o' people have funny notions about our boys. A banker once thought of them as you did. When they got him in here and cropped his head and put a grey uniform on him he looked about like the rest. A little more stupid, maybe. But do you know he never did get over it. He strutted around here all decorated with invisible privileges as proud as a peacock, pretending to sicken at the other boys' crimes. He came in with a one-to-ten sentence for betraying the trust of his friends, working folks mostly, and widows. Got away with two hundred and fifty thousand. But the boys weren't much hurt by his opinions. They're tolerant towards those *without sin*. They kinda like the cartoons people make of them. Any kind of attention is better than none. They even like the stones of the pious—more so than the hymns, I reckon."

He goes on to inform us that the population of any major prison is made up mostly of old offenders, two-three, and four-time losers; and that except for their criminal tendencies they are a fair cross section of American citizenry at its best, its average, and its worst. Here are educated men and ignorant men. Here you may find the giant and the dwarf; the morally strong and the morally weak; men of many nations, trades, crafts, professions. Here is the cunning man with narrow eyes and loose underlip. Here, too, is the stupid dolt with dull eyes and a perpetual grin. You will discover spiritual men in prison, psychics, mediums, sensitives, cultists, and the various variety of *deified* freaks, wearing imaginary haloes and communicating with imaginary hosts celestial. Here you will discover the inflated Ego around whom is gathered a ring of yes men, or shadows, as they are called in prison. The atheist is here with his incessant preachment; the agnostic with his claim to realism; the cynic with his superficial rationalism; the sceptic with his affected boredom. All are here.

There are doddering old criminals and beardless, naive ones, the latter making heroes of the former. There are scholars who can point out how the invention of an Eskimo pie affected international trade; economists who can trace recurring depressions back to the causes which overthrew the Roman Empire. Here there are scientists, genuine and pseudo; inventors at work on the burglar-proof lock, and artists in all phases of development and defeat; prison poets and historians who interpret the trends in penal evolution. Here you will find the feverish genius busy with the perfect crime and the flawless escape plot. The financier is here with his too obvious grief and inevitable soft job, as well as his oft-repeated promise "to pay back every cent." The lawyer is here, now serving without a retainer, the many who seek his legal advice. He still continues to plead his own cause and to close up the holes in his forgotten case. Here is the weak-chinned and polished confidence man who intends to do it differently the next time. Here you will find the zealot with a foolproof social order; the religious fanatic who knows how to lock all the doors of hell and bind Satan for a thousand years, or who, out of the grey ranks, searches for the *elect*, who will join the hundred and forty-four thousand on the "last day" to receive the crown of immortal life, body and all. You will discover in prison the ex-minister who dispatched his wife or rival because of his inordinate affection. Here are saintly men and terrible sinners, the good and the bad, the reasonably pure and the unreasonably degenerate.

It is, to a great extent, the picture of humanity. However, here in the prison melting pot the actors have all been levelled, the barriers of caste and position have vanished, and they have all scurried into the shuffling regiment of numbers.

Someone speaks of the terrible sacrifice these men have made for the dubious profits from crime.

"There are always compensations for sacrifice," our guide says. "Women had to sacrifice their appeal with their clothes and men's illusions. It ain't been such a bad exchange. They've got used to their vanished magnetism. Our boys get used to their vanished freedom."

With this philosophic observation, we follow our escort back to the iron steps and in a few moments the prison is behind us.

CHAPTER 2

THE VERDICT OF MEN

Truly, the best wisdom of man is as foolishness to God. To the ablest in worldly wisdom the ways of God are past finding out.

Many men have stated, many more have implied of me, "Yours is a hopeless case." At least four of these were well qualified to speak. They had the best of the lesser light. There was integrity in their judgment. The lesser integrity. From this point I can both admire their candour and commiserate with it.

I have in mind a Trial Judge. At the time, criminally hardened as I was, I believe I felt a tinge of affection and sadness for him. I know he meant well. He was an unhappy man. His private and family life enlivened the daily rounds of jail routine. They were made the subject for cheap gossip and tawdry pastime. Had he been aware of our remarks, I'm sure his professional dignity would have been wounded. Out of his tragedy we collected soggy threads and wove them into a pattern for killing time. From its inception, the story went, his home had been a breeding place for sorrow and heartbreaking disappointment. Because of this he drank too much. But the only local criticism seemed to be, "Who could blame him?"

He wore a mask, which even I could see through. He had fashioned it out of pain and pretence. His poker face and austere manner were too obviously affected. Behind them beat the heart of a born sentimentalist.

There was a rumour that he had wanted to be a doctor. Whether of divinity or medicine we didn't learn. His parents chose the legal profession for him. He had done well in it. He must have made them proud in his success. He had justified their hopes and the money they had spent on him to make their wishes come true. His crucifixion had been slow, leaving room for many acts of genuine charity and mercy, many rich displays of nobler understanding. As a defending lawyer he had shared the happiness his talents had brought to others. Later, as one who judged others, he had shared their miseries. In this latter position, save for his drinking, he had carried his cross with patience and courage.

On the edge of my teens I had my first encounter with the law. This man, then a young lawyer, recently admitted to the bar, defended me. His skill saved me from a trip to Reform School. My victory was followed by a couple of decades in crime, most of which time I spent in one prison or another. Once more we met in a courtroom. I was there to answer for a major crime. This time his role was reversed. He was not present to defend but to condemn me. He performed his duty with the usual gravity, which was supposed to become a man on the bench. After passing sentence, an indeterminate one, my third to a major prison, and my last, he went beyond the requirements of legal duty and added his own personal opinion.

"I know you are sick," he said solemnly. "And I know that more punishment is not the remedy. There is something wrong in our system of dealing with men like you. I don't know what it is. Your record leaves us powerless. Our helplessness is your hopelessness."

I know he was sincere in his verdict and opinion. With sadness and reluctance he gave the verdict. As I recall the incident now my thoughts bridge the chasm of two thousand years, and I can see Jesus with His desire to gather wayward Jerusalem as a hen gathereth her brood. And they would not! Could this judge, at this moment, have touched me with the magic hand of healing it would have made him glad. His manner affected me that way. But, like Jerusalem with Jesus, I would have none of his redeeming power. I had not yet suffered

30

enough. My soul was not yet ripe for plucking. The harvest was still green. The winnowing and the screening would come later. I needed more pain, much more. As surely as ignorance rejected the healing power of the Master Healer, I rejected the words of this judge who, behind his mask, had my best interest genuinely at heart.

I have come to believe in a destiny running through the crazy pattern of my life. In this destiny I have reserved a special place for this particular Trial Judge. For my first infraction of the law he defended me: for my last he sentenced me. He was with me at the beginning of my criminal career: he was with me at the finish. This may be a coincidence. But then again it may not be. If it is not, the good Judge may appear in a future chapter of my story, though his spirit has long ago raced away to that realm where judgment "is mine saith the Lord." At least I want to believe that this judge had an influence for good in my life.

Again I am thinking of a certain prison warden. He was a practical penologist, who mixed his severe discipline with a raw meat brand of justice. His ambition was to be uniformly harsh. It infuriated him and outraged his character when he was forced to bow before some political pet in prison, who had been committed to him with a recommendation for special privileges. In other words, for coddling.

He loathed his own stool pigeon system, which he lacked wisdom to correct or eliminate. He detested the weaklings who curried his favour in return for tainted information. He once sent me to the "hole" on the secret and doubtful evidence of one of his numerous informers.

"You've been snitched on," he told me bluntly.

"I know it," was my reply.

"Are you guilty?" he asked.

"No," I answered.

"Do you mean my stool pigeon is a liar?"

"And a long-tailed rat," I said, knowing I was sunk anyway.

"In this sewer it takes a rat to trap a rat," he said caustically. "I'm not in love with either brand, you know."

"That's why you're admired in here, warden," I replied, honestly.

He looked at me steadily for a moment. "How would you like to know the stool's name who squawked on you?" he asked.

"You've got to depend on your stool pigeons, warden. But you don't have to become one yourself."

"That's a good answer," he replied. "Because you've done well, I'll give you ten days instead of fifteen. While you're doing the ten you can hate me all you want. I won't mind. For I'll forget you the minute you walk out of here. The hate you'll wallow in over there will punish you more than the bread and water. I'll appreciate your cooperation."

No doubt there is much in the life of a prison official with which the toughest convict may sympathize, for he, too, has been caught in a vicious programme of life. For a man with an innate desire to administer fair and impartial treatment, a prison job is no bed of roses. He must seek and accept the favours of men whom his very nature holds in contempt. Such was the character and position of this warden.

For thirty years he had looked steadily upon the faults of others. His own faults had become obscured to him. His most recurrent comment was, "My illusions about the goodness in men are gone." He always said it as though in self-justification of his betrayed desires. He had made judgment his ideal as well as his duty and he had come to believe firmly in appearances, the very stuff out of which every convict weaves his false beard, and back of which he hides the perpetual war in his soul.

I hated this warden enormously. However, I could admire his good though futile intentions to treat all prisoners alike. I held him in a morbid sort of respect. This attitude was general. In effect his verdict of me was that my end was certain. Either my criminal career would be stopped in a blaze of violence, or I would wind it up somewhere in a prison cell.

The third man was the chairman of our parole board. He had been made the unwitting victim of a grim trick of destiny. An academic idealist, he was unsuited to a post he owed to one of the periodic waves of newspaper protest against corruption in the parole department. The job threw him out of character and ruined him. He came too soon and left too late. Great was the price he paid for experience. He traded sentiment for cynicism, his ideals for a surface realism, his faith in man for doubt. My record proved to him that I was beyond correction.

And the fourth man was a resident prison psychiatrist. He was popular behind the walls. A young good-looking fellow, his smooth face and fresh vitality gave a lift to jaded appetites. He had come to his position direct from college. His copybook aura had not yet been tinged with dull professionalism. He became the subject for much prison humour and gossip. There was a story out that he wore a gentleman's corset, a rumour which, because of the dignity of his official position, he could neither affirm nor deny. The convicts referred more often to his figure than to his ability.

By being honest I received an adverse verdict from him. It was on the occasion of his giving me a mental test. Among the questions with which he confronted me was the following: "If you were walking through the woods and you came upon a man hanging from a limb by the neck, what would you do?"

"I'd first go through his pockets," I replied. "Then I'd make my getaway." He was displeased with my answer, telling me that it was not only incorrect but facetious.

"The first thing you would do," he explained, "would be to ascertain whether the man was still alive or dead. If alive you would take him down. If dead you would leave him hanging. In either case you would go speedily to notify the proper authorities."

He was unable to appreciate the convict point of view. I was unable to appreciate the official point of view. Between these two extremes there was a connecting link, but neither of us knew what it was. I maintained that such an act on my part would be inconsistent;

that no real criminal would go to the authorities of his own free will; that I had always made the authorities come to me; and that there could be no point in my ascertaining life or death in the hanging man. For this defence of my point of view, he wrote behind my name and number: "A chronic recidivist. Criminal insanity present. Perhaps a borderline case." A convict friend of mine in the parole office told me about the damaging notation. I got an audience with the young mental expert, flattered him a little, told him I had pondered the test question, and could now see that I was wrong and that he was right. The notation was altered to read: "Antisocial personality. Conduct and behaviour unpredictable." This was less menacing. He had changed the phrasing without destroying his passion for words.

Perhaps the real difficulty confronting prison psychiatry is a matter of penetration. It may yet be discovered that the basic cause of crime is a problem for the soul surgeon rather than the mental scientist.

At any rate, as it turned out, all these authorities were wrong. Their verdicts were justified, but not vindicated. To them the ways of God were not considered. For my ultimate correction society is not indebted to man, but to Providence.

CHAPTER 3

IN DEFENCE OF MAN'S VERDICT

A FRIEND, AFTER READING THIS CHAPTER IN MANUSCRIPT, reproved me on the ground that the material was morbid. He said the psychology was too personal and too heavy. The reader, he thought, might accuse me of unnecessarily exploiting very delicate personal matters for the sake of building up sensational effects.

"Why stretch yourself upon a cross?" he asked.

"I have no desire for sensational effects," I replied, "but I have a deep conviction that my readers have a right to know my background, my past attitude, and through me the viewpoint of the confirmed criminal. My authority to speak is experience and not scholarship. My sins of commission have purpose. Omission of them in a document of this nature would defeat that purpose, cheat the reader of clarifying information, and thus reduce me to a literary burglar; the last estate being little better than the first."

Because I have faith in the tolerance and judgment of anyone who has read this far, I will present a compact record of the man whom the prison system failed to correct.

My earliest memory is that of fear; three fears, and the greatest of these was sin. As a child my nature was painfully religious. I quailed before sin in others. My own sins would torture me for days on end. The other two fears to which I had been heir were likewise of the sort which are endured alone, for to confide them was to court ridicule. I feared the very mention of death. The thought of going to sleep was unbearable because it was haunted by the fear of never waking. And I had a horrifying fear of finding myself locked in, with no way of escape from the dangers my vivid imagination would conjure up.

From this latter fear I suffered through all my criminal career. Though I spent many years behind locked doors, the persistence of this fear remained active behind my mask and would often recur to torment my nights.

My early childhood was compensated, however, by beautiful spiritual dreams. In these Jesus walked and talked. These dreams were most vivid and captivating when my fear of going to sleep was most intense. They seemed to visit me as a sort of balancing grace, a reassurance concerning the sleep state, as though they were trying to tell me that there was nothing to fear.

I didn't get very far in school. The fifth grade stopped education. My interest was vague. My power of concentration was poor, and I had a deplorable memory. This latter fault had much to do with my later life. In my schooldays we had monthly recitations, which were stumbling blocks for me, since the memorizing of lines was difficult.

When I was eight, the thing happened which so adversely affected my future. For three weeks my sister had laboured to pound a four-verse poem into my head before recitation day. When the time came I felt confident. The school room was crowded with visitors, mostly the mothers of those who would speak their pieces. I am sure I felt a little pang of disappointment because no one was there to support me with a reassuring smile, no one to take pride in my histrionic talents, or to share my triumph. That is, no one from my own family. There was a stepmother, but she was too busy to come; my father was at work. I recall distinctly that I wished for the face of my own mother among the others.

By and by when my turn came I arose and walked boldly to the platform. I faced the audience proudly and began with assurance. But at midway I forgot the key line. I fidgeted awkwardly, trying to remember. It was no use. My face was burning with embarrassment.

Then some child giggled. In an instant the whole room was filled with laughter, which the teacher tried to stem, while choking back her own impulse to laugh. I ran from the room as one mortally wounded, terribly ashamed. My first fight came as a result of this fiasco.

I have pondered this childhood situation in the light of another exactly like it, which came in adulthood. I ran away from it in exactly the same way, feeling the same cutting sense of embarrassment and shame. The first situation was not conquered by running. Neither was the second. And the thought has often come to me that there are certain tests in our lives, problems, which recur again and again, perhaps in a little different garb, until we face them and conquer them in the right way. Then the experience disappears to make room for a higher and better experience.

The outcome of my running away from this childhood test or experience, and the effort to conquer the aftereffects by violence, planted my young feet on the path that was to lead me into crime. It caused me to dislike boys of my own age, and to seek the society of older boys. This abnormal process kept up until at twelve I had left the world of boyhood and had attached myself to the world of men. I was but a boy with a man's mind. The virtues of men had not developed in me; but I found it comparatively easy to win their fellowship by simply copying their vices. This, of course, was dangerous, since the vices of men were motivated by passion, while organically I was still a child of innocence. Later on, after I had advanced deeply into manhood I was a creature of intensity still acting upon the impulses of innocence.

This is the twist in character that makes the criminal. It is one thing to act in an antisocial way while still on the childhood side of puberty. Society is prone to be patient with a child's impulses. The same acts, however, committed with passion, become criminal. And most confirmed criminals are men who act upon the impulses of their early childhood.

The vices I copied were chiefly gambling, pool-playing, drinking. I was twelve when I took my first drink. At thirteen I had my first alcoholic baptism. After that the liquor road was easy. The next step led me into stealing.

In my early teens I was a major criminal. In the hideouts and jungle-camps of the country I fraternized with thieves and fugitives, whose records were long and whose deeds were as black as a Stygian Hell. With eagerness I looked forward to the day when my record, too, would be long and black; when I would have a reputation among my kind as a dangerous man; when the police would refer to me with a shudder, and when the deadliest criminal would pay me the respect that cowardice pays to physical pain. Mine was the left-handed ambition of the budding outlaw.

I soon became adapted to the underworld. Thoroughly inured to its vulgarity and shameless profanity, its merciless philosophy, I moved from crime to crime and from jail to jail, always ready to adopt the worst and to repulse the best in human nature.

There were many who sought to help me; good men and women reaching toward me with a selfless hand. But they were naive in their proffered kindness, untrained in the subtle psychology of the criminal mind. There were officers of the law who, being disarmed by my apparent innocence and youthfulness, by my acting and my gift of clever deception, many times sacrificed duty to indulgence, permitting me to go scot-free to repeat my offences and to ply my trade. They thought they were giving me a chance to make good. They were, in fact, contributing to my weakness and not to my latent strength. Too, there were juvenile authorities who listened to my penitential tales. By misplaced mercy they betrayed the society who looked to them for protection and who buttered their daily bread.

And there were the voluntary, unskilled social workers who mistook a maudlin sentimentalism for a divine mission. They were called "sob sisters." As a usual thing they were frustrated and inhibited in their emotional parts. They had no well-defined theory concerning the correction of wayward boys, as they referred to them. As for wayward women, for some unknown reason, they seemed to have little interest. Many of them had mothering complexes, which "the boys" were inclined to play up to, calling them Mother So-and-So. I am sure they did some good, if for no other reason than the fact that the prison officials resented their missionary labours. Of course, they were taken advantage of on occasion and were used to "square a rap," in the jargon of crime, when a guilty criminal, through their influence, had his case dismissed. I always knew I should have them for my friends if, perchance, my crime and arrest were sufficiently notorious to merit headlines. If there were no other reason, this fact alone would keep me charitably disposed toward the so-called "sob sisters." When the whole world is belching out venom against a man it takes at least courage to speak out in his behalf.

But despite the laudable intentions of all these good people I am compelled to say that they fed my criminal ego rather than my sleeping soul.

Prisons, jails, penal farms, chain-gangs, the third degrees of the police world—the whole sordid and futile programme of punishment did its best to straighten out my twisted character. And it failed. Instead of theocentric it made me increasingly egocentric. All for the simple reason that I didn't want to be corrected! Only God can help the man who has no desire to help himself.

Neither did the more modern prison experiments help me any. I was in the world to take advantage of society, to exploit those whom I considered my natural enemies. If an attempt at kindness was shown me it released two responses: *first*, I looked upon every such gesture with suspicion, as something spurious, a counterfeit with a selfish motive behind it, a trick of some kind; *second*, I held it my duty to turn the tables and to outwit such persons to my own benefit. With this attitude I naturally defeated every effort intended as an aid to my best interest.

As the old prison system of contract labour and unqualified brutality gave way to the modern trend of experimental penology, the resident prison psychiatrist became an official cog in the new wheel. He, too, tried to bring a glimmer of light into my dark skull. Did he succeed where others had failed? Not at all. My reaction to him was that of every confirmed criminal, most uncharitable. His tedious rigmarole of *case-histories* was looked upon as a smokescreen hiding a soft and lucrative job, and an attempt to dignify with the air of science a new kind of racket. I resented his question-and-answer system. I considered it an impudent piece of probing into my private affairs. I figured that he was using me to deceive a gullible tax-paying public, who had been awed into believing that science could correct criminals and solve the crime problem. I was nauseated by his professional atmosphere. I loathed what I thought to be his expressed and unexpressed judgment of me, and used his unconvincing effort at friendliness to hold him up to ridicule before all impressionable first offenders. I could have been greatly helped by several prison psychiatrists if I had had one decent brain cell working. I can see that now, but then I was crime-blinded. Intelligent self-interest had no place in my life.

The day came when the harsh disciplines of the old prison system yielded to the modern trend toward laxity as a corrective device in the New Penology. It had no good effect on my cynical and case-hardened character. On the contrary I hated it, because it made conversation and mixing among convicts too easy. It came as a boon to those who gathered information and peddled it to the officials in return for favours. It simplified the news-gathering tactics of the stool pigeons, and worked against those who preferred silence and secrecy. I could have been helped in many constructive ways by this more humane method if I had had any desire for self-improvement, but with my attitude it only served to open up new fields of iniquity in an already degraded personality.

Then there was the new device of occupational therapy, which was calculated to stimulate pride in workmanship, release incentive, and stir up ambition. Also, it was intended to prepare us for a life of honest industry after our prison terms had expired. But crime was my incentive and ambition. The old habituals were busy preparing themselves for their next crime; not for an honest position in the outside world. I could have been greatly assisted by this method if I had wanted to seize upon the opportunity it offered. But it had no salutary effect in my life.

I was tortured, cajoled, persuaded, and I continued a criminal in thought and feeling and action.

Not even the splendid, though indulgent, love of my father had any good effect on the kind of life I had chosen to lead. For years he spent time and energy and money trying to keep me out of jail. Because of me he lost his reputation for being a man of sound judgment and robust good sense. Because of me he sacrificed his friends; he became a laughing stock, an object of pity, but he kept his faith in me.

It now appears significant that as a young man my father had been called to the ministry, and that he had refused to heed that call. He had tried vainly to let it go. But at no time in his life had it let him go. He had to learn by bitter experience that to act contrary to the guidance of intuition was to take the pain-path of compulsion instead of the path of grace and gladness. All his laborious escape efforts were made the more blistering by their utter inability to stifle that "still, small voice" of his deeper and finer self. The last sad touch to this self-produced tragedy was a sense of guilt. He was convinced that by his example he had become an accessory to my crimes. He, too, had travelled a side road. He, too, had carried the wrong cross.

I remember a long and miserable tussle he had with liquor, another of his escape devices that would not work; long hours and even days of remorse, anxiety, self-condemnation, feelings of helplessness and impotence, the incessant struggle against the example he was setting, the misery of repeated failures, of resolutions made and defeated. And finally there was the conquest of drink by the frightful force of a desperate will, which left him still unsatisfied with his victory. This caused him a lingering suspicion that though suppressed, the habit had not been correctly or wholly conquered. There was the subtle but real fear that in some future crisis the bottle would once more offer him the way out, that he would first indulge and then succumb. His victory had not been gained the God way.

But because of his faith in me my father went about among influential politicians pleading for help to get me out of prison, begging them to write letters of recommendation. Always his persistence was rewarded by the furthering of my weakness. It was thus rewarded on the occasion of my next to last prison sentence. I was released prematurely because of it. He came all the way to the prison to meet me and to share my joy of freedom. As we rode away together he spoke quietly of his faith in my future. He related one of the principal reasons for this—my mother.

My mother had been a beautiful woman with a sensitive nature and a tender conscience. God was ever her delight and fortress. She lived in His presence. Within a few weeks after the light of my life began to shine, that of my mother was extinguished. My father mentioned that I was a sacrificial child. I know he wanted to impress me with this fact, to arouse in me a sense of appreciation of it. He went on to say that my mother believed that there was a good destiny in store for me because of her sacrifice in giving me birth. Hence, at her deathbed and as her last request, I was to have my chance.

Without even an accent of preachment my father said to me as we journeyed along: "So you see, son, I want you to make good. Not for my sake, but to realize the faith your mother had in you."

And while he talked I was meditating upon my next crime.

To add to his disappointment, I went to the little town of my birth to commit this crime. Here my sister lived with her husband and children. Already the shadow of my disgrace had fallen across their world. This final blow emphasized the extent of my perfidious indifference to others, my crass and wholly indefensible selfishness. In this village I was caught redhanded burglarizing a store.

The next morning my father heard the news. He came immediately to the jail. He had aged twenty years in two hours. His great heart was at last broken. But not his faith! It still burned in his dim, tear-misted eyes, now glazed with a nameless, measureless pain. He put his hands through the bars and held mine. His own felt dry and hot and withered. He could not trust himself to speak for a long time. He just stood there in muted agony, his head half-bowed, his eyes avoiding mine, his body bent as though beneath an impossible cross. He had to suffer in silence. Out of it emerged no word of condemnation. He was alone with his own and my suffering, two diametrically opposite kinds of pain, the one unselfish, Christlike, the other generated by self-accusation and self-resentment for getting caught. When the jailer called to him that his time was up, he spoke briefly, "It's all right, son. I'll not cover up my own blame. Somewhere, in some way, it will all be made right, maybe." With this he turned away.

He came to the depot to bid me a last farewell as, handcuffed, I boarded the train to begin what was destined to be my final prison sentence—a destiny as strange and unexpected, as it was beautiful. He had no perception of the wonderful grace I was approaching, nor of the terrifying torture. Yet he spoke prophetically. "I'll not live to see you again. As a young man I was called to the ministry. I ignored my calling. I hope you won't miss yours."

• • •

I never saw my father again, but I believe with all my heart that he entered a new and finer dimension of life. And I want to believe that he is glad because he kept the faith when only one other person on earth believed in my recovery. I want to believe that both my father and mother are rejoicing in my struggle along the dusty, rough road that is leading back toward God.

However, I was returned to prison the same old hate-bitten criminal. Only now I was obsessed with a consuming passion, a mad and sinister purpose.

CHAPTER 4

THE PROBLEM OF
THE OLD OFFENDERS

A FEW YEARS AGO ONE OF AMERICA'S FOREMOST PENOLOGISTS made an astonishing confession in print. In effect he said: "We are interested in the first offenders. Nothing can be done for the old habitual criminals anyway."

His words are astonishing because of their hopeless pessimism and utter futility. It is generally conceded among the authorities that the old offenders constitute the major menace of crime. If nothing can be done by the prison system toward correcting them, then society is indeed in an unfortunate position, and is faced with the danger of eventual criminal rule. For the ranks of the old offenders, if not decreased by the prison system, must inevitably increase in spite of it—if not because of it.

The percentage of corrections among first offenders is not available, but this is certain: every first offender who is not corrected by the prison system becomes an old offender. Personal experience and observation have revealed to me that a year in prison, the most abnormal environment in the world, is just as likely to confirm as it is to heal the beginning criminal. If he has sufficient strength of character, nothing the prison can do for or against him will make much difference. He will check off his months, go out, and return no more. But if his conscience is blunted and his character weak, everything connected with prison life, both good and bad, is likely to contribute to his further degradation, convince him that he was born to crime, and thus furnish him with an excuse for antisocial conduct rather than with an incentive to strive, struggle, and believe in his inherent possibilities and essential goodness.

I agree with the penologist, however, that nothing can be done for the old offender—by the prison system alone. In fact, my experience of many years in prison contains no record of a single confirmed criminal who was corrected only by punitive methods. *On the other hand, my memory is crowded with confirmed criminals who were healed while in prison. In every case this was accomplished through the power of religion.*

I have often wondered how different it would be if Christ were warden, or even if our prisons were supplied with chaplains who really understood the psychology of the convict mind and were helped by official cooperation rather than hindered by interference toward the establishment of a genuine prison religion, framed to fit the special need of those who live in a different world. A gospel calculated to feed conventional and socially-minded people could hardly be expected to find much favour among those who are unconventional and antisocial.

Prison religion is the square peg in a round hole.

But in spite of the fact that most chaplains are untrained and inadequate, and that prison religion speaks to convicts in an unknown tongue, it is the one and only power behind prison walls which can and does redeem the hardened old offender.

But let us return to that cell house we recently inspected. There is a long, straight path of boards, flanked on the outside by an iron railing and on the inside by a stone face in which has been left a string of square holes and barred doors. It is the second of four tiers up. Its name: "Receiving gallery."

Behind one of these barred doors is an almost barren cell. Here is where the convict begins his stretch. The impressionable first offender may be made or broken during the two or three days he is confined in one of these receiving cells.

I should say that the greatest opportunity offered the prison system to make a lasting impression on the life of a first offender is to be found on this receiving gallery. Alone in one of these drab, bare cells the unhardened new arrival is certain to become pensive and reflective. The conscience pricks him into shame and grief. Thoughts of his crime press in upon him. He thinks of his parents, friends, relatives, and of the disgrace and sorrow his misdeed has brought to these dear ones. Still tender and responsive to the finer sentiments, he is likewise pervious to constructive sympathy and wise understanding. If ever the touch of Christ was needed in the life of a first offender it is when he finds himself in a cell on the receiving gallery—alone with his thoughts and feelings in a strange, abnormal environment—face to face with his conscience on the one hand and the threatening terrors of prison life on the other, both of which he is apt to magnify out of all proportion.

Vividly I recall this situation in my career of crime. I am convinced now, and always have been, that my criminal activities, even with the start I had, could have been ended on the first day and night I spent in the cell of a major prison. Had I heard the right voice then, I am certain that society would have been saved a mountainous toll, and I many years of bitterness and wasted life.

But whose was the first voice to reach me? A stupid guard who jeered at my fear and grief; a keeper who leaned against my cell door and taunted and mocked and menaced me; a free man who sought to wear away my self-control; a paid attendant who tried to infuriate me into an act of insolence, so that he might have an excuse for reporting me and thus getting me started off on the wrong foot. He did arouse my anger and hatred, but he failed to topple my self-control. The hate he invoked in me was so violent that it absorbed all my fears and griefs, along with all my good impulses and intentions.

The next voice I heard was that of a convict who was in charge of this, the most important of all the galleries from the standpoint of official opportunity. But who was this fellow in charge? And how could such a man secure this kind of job? The receiving gallery being the least populated, it became at once the softest of the cell house jobs. Favours have to be shown and special privileges given to stool pigeons, the lowest and foulest of men who feed upon the misfortunes of their own kind. And this fellow, a stool pigeon and degenerate, had thus been favoured with a resultant cost to society in bloodshed, rape, and money beyond any possible computation.

He was a five-time loser to prison; was utterly without conscience or a sense of responsibility. He, too, made sordid pastime out of my predicament, and sought to influence me in all the pernicious ways familiar to him. In bland, confidential tones he told me how to "do" time—but not a word of how to "use" time. During my stay on the receiving gallery this man gave me a thorough education in the deadly convict philosophy of life. I swallowed it. And there was not a word of it which was not aimed at my destruction at society's expense.

On a blustery February afternoon I was in a cell on the receiving gallery. I was now booked as an habitual criminal facing the maximum of a twenty-year sentence. Hatred, dissipation, poor liquor, and prison punishment had written their raw history in my body. My vital organs were shot. My nervous system was at the point of collapse. Already a prematurely old man as I sat in my cell that afternoon and night, my thoughts were not of shame and disgrace, for I had been divorced from conscience. Rather I was filled and seared with a crimson hatred and black rebellion. I hated everything and everybody, including myself.

Looking down the calendar of those penalizing years, and measuring them against my physical condition, I found three courses open to me: *first*, I could try to maintain a good prison record with the vague hope of outliving the devastating term; *second*, I could take the way of self-destruction; *third*, I could set my mind and ingenuity on escape.

After a moment's reflection, the first course was promptly rejected. What sort of a wreck would I be at the end of this long stretch? A feeble, worn-out prison lag; a silly old stir bug going about muttering ineffectually to myself; a broken, quacking member of the prison's crank gang. I would be released an impotent old "has been" with no stamina left to commit a decent crime. And I would wind up either a bloodless and spineless bread-and-butter beggar, or would deliberately let myself be caught in the act of committing some cheap offence and come whimpering back to end my days in prison, to pledge my bones to the prison graveyard.

The second course, suicide, had its appeal. It was counteracted, however, by the inherent logic of the third course, and by the remark of a fellow convict. He had called it the coward's way out. It took courage to face the music; none to knife the fiddler!

In escape there was nothing to lose. There was freedom to gain. At that time I knew nothing of freedom, of what it was or what it meant. Just to be on the other side of prison walls was what I took to be freedom. A fugitive from justice, slinking through the shadows, dodging the eyes of my natural enemies, hunted by day and hounded by night—this was the grand prize for which I would make my bid and stake my life! I therefore made my resolution. I would try. If I failed I would pay the fierce price and try it again. Again, again, and again I would try. I would stop trying only at the point where my mind was shattered and my body was broken.

Now that I had cut my knots and was firmly resolved upon my future course of action the plan began to take form in my twisted brain and bitter heart. Had I known what was ahead of me I could not have faced it. I was to press my life into the last black niche of hell on earth.

Against this ebony background an unearthly light was to break on my consciousness, and I was to know the full joy and meaning concealed in the sublime word, FREEDOM.

CHAPTER 5

OFF THE RECORD

I MADE THREE DESPERATE BIDS FOR FREEDOM, OR WHAT I THEN thought to be freedom. Two of these attempts were of the "lone wolf" variety. The third involved group action, destruction of state property, and physical violence.

After four days on the receiving gallery, I was assigned to work as a shovel man in the rock quarry. My warder was an old-timer in prison work who was best known as "Hawk Eye." His lack of education and his inability to govern men by intelligence had kept him from advancing. He had an unending desire to assert his superior place as master and to make the convict realize his inferior place as slave. Outside of a few pets he heartily disliked all prisoners, and this sentiment was just as heartily reciprocated.

I knew of Hawk Eye and of his reputation. He knew of me and mine. I had never before taken his orders, for I had always managed to keep out of his gang. Now that I was assigned to his quarry I decided to use diplomacy and a strong-willed patience. I would rigorously choke back protest and revolt and guard myself against being trapped by him into a rash display of insolence, with its consequent trip to solitary for a period on bread and water.

He was gloating when I reported myself for duty. "Well, well," he said, chuckling, "if it ain't the old prison-born baby come back. So you couldn't make it outside, eh? Got hungry for some more of our good stew. Well, you won't have to go hungry for a long time. You'll get the works this trip. That might be a temptation to you, eh? It might make you want to take a chance. I wouldn't do it if I was you. It might not be safe even to play with the idea."

His warning was plain enough. The word had gone out to keep an eye on me, and his was a sharp eye.

I ignored Hawk Eye's advice about playing with the idea.

I began to do a lot of thinking, but not out loud. The first thing I thought about was the prison's weakest spot. The second thing had to do with the human equation. How far could I go alone? In whom could I confide? In whom could I trust after I had reached the end of my own resources?

One thing was certain: I was committed to the purpose of escape. The plan began to take form when I asked myself: "How?" The time of my escape was easily decided upon. It would be at night when the encircling walls were free of guards. I would cut my way into the prison yard and scale the wall under cover of darkness. This involved the matter of obtaining a hacksaw blade, and it was at this point where I must seek the aid of confederates. I decided, however, to run the risk. And this brought me to the next step in my march to liberty, that of place.

Here I had a choice between the cell house and the prison hospital. Having to choose the point of least resistance, the cell house with its double-barred protection and vigilant night watch was ruled out promptly. Obviously the hospital with an outside window to every sick room, with its three floors, and with only one warder and night nurse on duty, was the weak spot in the prison. It was, in fact, more difficult for me to get into it than to get out of it.

Mentally I went over the list of my prison pals in search of the one who could be trusted to aid me. There was Fighting Jack Donovan, an old underworld friend of mine. There was Smiler Wallace, and an old buddy called Tommy Gun. There was Dago John and Yorkie and the Denver Wop. Pickhandle Charlie Gibson was there. And finally there was LongShot Jim Harmer.

I had done a number of favours for Jim. I could trust him, too. He would have money if it were needed, for besides being the best moneymaking tinkerer in the place he was an expert gambler.

I confided my need of a hacksaw to him one day on the recreation ground.

"That's a cinch," he said. "If a brier was all that stood between me and the street I'd a' been out of this joint long ago. Curly Morgan's over there in the pipe shop, you know. Curly and me's just like that." He held up two closely pressed fingers. "Cell house?" he asked.

"Hospital," I replied.

"Don't make me laugh," he cut back. "You'll never get inside that joint until they're ready to wash you for your last suit and a free ride out the back gate."

"Can you get the brier to me if I do make it?" I asked.

"Sure," he affirmed. "If you can get in I'll do the rest. What's the dodge, a phony fit?"

"Soap," I replied.

He looked at me with unbelief in his gaze. "That's slow suicide. Remember Bugs Allen? He took that route, you know. He's up there in the bone yard now. He got in the hospital, all right, when he was half dead. And he didn't come out until they lugged him out. An ounce of this con soap would croak a mule."

That evening I began my soap diet, taking a very small amount at first, with the view of affecting a gradual decline. In a few days I started to haunt the morning sick-call complaining to the doctor of stomach trouble. And each morning I would get a dose of salts or a packet of pills. As I increased the amount of soap taken, its corrosive effects became more violent, and I began to suffer the proverbial agonies of the damned. It seemed as though my whole insides were on fire. My stomach was inflamed, and a red-hot ball of fire lay at its pit. I was suffering repeated attacks of terrifying nausea. But the nearest I came to getting into the hospital was the morning I fell out while standing in the sick-call line. The doctor called the Captain of the Guard to one side and conversed with him about me. The result was not the hospital but undisturbed confinement in my cell, alone!

When the deputy warden came down to see me I protested.

"You're not kidding anybody," was his reply.

"You may get away with this and you may not," I said. "I still have people outside, you know. They might get curious and cause an investigation some day. Even though you keep them away from me now, the books will tell this story." I was bluffing, but he did not know it.

"We'll be ready for it when it comes. From now on you're off the record. We keep a punishment record to show the parole board. We don't need to bother with that in your case. You'll do all your time, anyway. And as far as the prison record goes, it will show you always at your work. Never, never under punishment."

If I had entertained any doubts about being marked for close observation and unusual punishment, they vanished with the deputy's words.

My plan had failed. That was certain. My hope now was to regain a sufficient measure of my health to warrant my being released from cell isolation. This was a slow and an excruciating process. I sought for every sort of means to divert my attention from the pains which constantly burned in my vitals, often doubling me up, like a jackknife, at which times my mouth would fill with hot and brackish water.

One day while steeling my will against what seemed to be an unbearable spasm of agony, my mental machinery became disorganized and I sank into a swoon-like condition. From physical pain I passed into a state of mental and emotional terror. I dreamed while I seemed wide awake. It was like a scroll or motion picture film, which began to unroll slowly before my vision. And the only pictures on it were the pictures of people I had injured. It seemed there would be no end to it. A vast number of these people I knew or had seen.

Then there were hundreds I had never seen. These were people who had been indirectly injured by me. The minute history of my long criminal career was thus relived by me, plus all the small injuries I had inflicted unconsciously by my thoughtless words and looks and omissions. Apparently nothing was omitted in this nightmare of injuries, but the most terrifying thing about it was that every pang of suffering I had caused others was now felt by me as the scroll unwound itself.

Then there came the horror of having to go through this experience again. It developed into a fear, which became a definite phobia, and which undoubtedly brought the thing I feared upon me. For this dream occurred to me no less than a dozen times during the next few weeks, in exactly the same way, and in the same detailed manner.

One morning I woke with a sense of well-being, quite free from pain and from fear. I had a feeling I would recover. From this time on my confinement was in the nature of convalescence. I did a great deal of thinking on the mystery and vagaries of the human mind. This was prompted by the experience I had passed through. Almost as though it were in response to this new interest, a book, which ordinarily would have held no interest for me, was tilted between the bars of my door by a fellow prisoner. It had been written by an oriental magician.

A chapter that seemed to grip me with a curious fascination dealt with the subject of being buried alive, and it described in detail just how the state was produced which made this feat possible. The state itself was arrested or suspended animation, a condition of coma, but much deeper than ordinary coma. It was produced by will power, preceded by a technical treatment of autosuggestion. This latter had to do with impressing upon the subconsciousness the exact time one wanted the state to end.

Perhaps I wasn't defeated after all in my purpose to get into the hospital. If, by practice and experiment, I could produce this coma, I had no doubt but that I would come to in a hospital bed. I did not succeed in my desire, but I did get myself into a mental state that was infinitely worse than the one I had previously been in. I was harassed by the continuous onslaughts of every fearsome creature and situation a distorted imagination was able to conjure up. This condition's nearest counterpart was delirium tremens, the result of protracted drinking.

When I was again in my right mind, I was still in my cell. I made no further attempts to gain admission to the hospital.

I spent four months in this isolation cell. I am grateful for that experience now, because it was a shadow cast before coming events, a dark shadow heralding a rosy new dawn! Here I discovered little-known continents in the human mind, mental outposts and frontiers, suggesting a land of indescribable promise beyond the desert of hate and fear and lust and greed. I was destined to reach this land, to experiment in the laboratory of the mind and spirit, to discover an area of unspeakable love, tranquillity, and a sanity so great and so simple as to cause one to wonder how poor bewildered and befuddled humanity could possibly have missed the way. *It was indeed the kingdom of heaven at hand.* And there was no conceit and futility in it. Truly, my isolation experience was but the muddled forecast of the freedom I sought as one who seeks amiss.

I was never returned to my job in the rock quarry. I was face to face with the scourge of every self-respecting convict, "assigned to the crank gang." So I had come to this! How many times I had laughed and sneered at these warped, half-crazy old prison lags, with their ceaseless whining, their futile whimpering, their childish displays of temper, idle gossip, and useless tantrums! The butt of crude jokes, caricatures of God's choicest creatures in whose presence even the foulest stool pigeon would sicken! Though a disciple of crime and an apostle of the convict philosophy of hate, I had arrived here, a member of the most detested and contempt-smeared body of men inside prison walls.

I was more determined than ever to escape. By now my hatred had overcome good judgment. I no longer shunned or feared violence. In the following months the plot grew. A dozen well-placed key men with a passion for liberty could turn the trick. To these key men the word was passed, and a three weeks' programme of agitation was under way.

The idea was to foment trouble among the impressionable and disgruntled convicts. The one raw spot in the penitentiary was the mess hall. Prison food was a constant source of suppressed discontent. Always it rankled beneath the surface of prison life. It was, in fact, the powder keg waiting for the wild-eyed maniac with a lighted match. This became our subject for agitation.

The plan was to excite the convicts into a grumbling protest, to set their nerves taut and on edge, to create an atmosphere of discontent, an air of sullen, brooding revolt and foreboding expectation. At the appointed time, which would be at the supper meal, this pent-up emotional dynamite would be touched off. An angry voice would cry out, a pan would bang the table, and in an instant the mob demon would be loosed in all its blind fury, ready to burn and kill and tear the prison to pieces. In the pandemonium those of us behind the plot would seize the deputy warden as a shield and hostage, menace him to the gate, and under threats of death force him to give the order that would swing the big gate open.

Something like a week had passed. Progress was being made by the spirit of agitation. Then suddenly the mumblings ceased. I, the leading actor in the plot, found myself in prison court to answer to a purely fictitious charge. I had been reported for an infraction of prison rules. I was told to state my case. I was not guilty, and I said so. This, of course, made a liar of the warder who had signed the report. It was understood that a warder was never wrong, and that the accused convict was never right.

As I faced my judge, the deputy warden, a prison man of the old school, an iron man whose illusions about convicts had vanished years before, I was filled with bitterness. First of all because my plot had been betrayed and thwarted by some stool pigeon who had exposed me as the leading spirit behind the agitation. And second because they had used this cheap means of disposing of me, an obvious frame-up. My hatred overbalanced reason and caused me to play into the deputy warden's hands. By refusing to admit my guilt I gave him the needed excuse for committing me to the dungeon. Once more I was "off the record." Whatever happened to me would never be read in black and white. I alone could tell the story—if I lived to give the details. But the record would prove my story a lie. It would show that during the time mentioned I was going serenely about my work in the prison "crank gang."

In committing me to the dungeon, the deputy added the following grim punch: "When I let you out you'll crawl to me on your knees and whine like a dog. And while you're in there eating bread and water, I'll be living on ham and eggs and sleeping in a good, warm bed."

I knew the warden meant what he said. On the other hand I knew I should never admit being guilty of this trumped-up charge. And above all, I knew that I would suffer death rather than crawl on my hands and knees, whining for release from the dungeon. What settled my fate, apparently, was the clashing of two human wills, unbreakable and uncompromising. It was a grim bargain. If outward appearances were to be considered and future possibilities ignored, I surely took the bad end of the deal. It is my present opinion that this crisis marked the ending of the first act of a soul's curious drama unfolded on the stage of destiny, and that the curtain was about to go up on the second act.

CHAPTER 6

GLORIFIED DARKNESS

OUT OF THE DARKNESS A SENSE OF DESTINY WAS BORN. I believe all men have a destiny, which is meaningless until it has emerged from the *sub*-nature and has become a motivating power in the *super*-nature. Further, I believe that all great men, men who have achieved vast things in a single lifetime, either for good or bad report, have been men who were ever aware of a driving destiny in their lives—men caught in the grip of a compelling and impelling power that would at no time let them go—and that their achievements have been commensurate with the feeling of destiny operating in their subjective lives.

When a man feels a sense of destiny in his life he manifests a courage and a spirit of adventure impossible to other men. What he undertakes he does with daring. He becomes a gambler who faces long odds with a feeling of inner assurance and protection. Self-consciousness and the pull of timidity, strong forces acting against success, are either overcome or nullified. He rises to opposition like a game fish to the fly, for instinctively he knows that his organic, mental and spiritual powers are released in direct proportion to the strength of the opposing force. Kagawa, the Japanese Christian, became aware of his destiny. He has sought and has overcome mountainous oppositions in his own nature and environment, and he has called himself "A gambler for God." The pages of history are replete with destiny-minded men and women, both as wreckers and builders on the world's stage.

I am prepared to state boldly that man will never determine his origin by looking backward, or by seeking his origin, but that he will find and know his origin only by looking forward, or by seeking his destiny.

In the light of the experience I shall soon recount, I can see the hand of destiny. Great was the opposition, great the power which overcame it. Without this light my life would remain a useless, senseless muddle with neither rhyme nor reason. If I have overcome the tug of habitual criminality during these eleven years in the outside world, I am indebted for that sustaining grace to the sense of destiny which was born in me at the point where I had fallen into the darkest pit of consciousness, into the lowest hell earth had to offer.

THE PRESENT

It is a square, solid structure, fashioned of dark grey limestone. Even to the casual visitor who is guided to its location there is a feeling of foreboding, as though the sombre stones are crying out against the outrages within.

Inside is a bare hall, save for an old desk and a tall pot bellied heating stove, which oozes smoke and exhales the fumes of coal sulphur, and which, when shaken and cleaned, sends out and up a dense barrage of fine, acrid ashes. The stove is there to keep the guard warm, for feeble, indeed, is its attempt to heat the dank, frostbitten building it occupies.

On each side of the enclosure are two rows of cells, one above the other. In front of each cell is a solid wooden door, in the centre of which is a covered peephole. Just behind this door is an inner one made of casehardened steel bars. The only light that filters into the cell comes from a small window set high in the outer wall, which is heavily barred on the inside, and which is covered by a thick iron grating on the outside. In one corner is a foul-smelling and battered waste bucket. This, with a quart tin cup, comprised the furnishings. In these dungeon cells the penalty is paid by him who dares to break the prison law.

It is winter time. The cells are cold and seeping moisture. The stone floor is damp and icy. The air has a dank density, like the interior of an old-fashioned icebox. I enter the place to begin my sentence in this black hell, wrought by man, God's choicest creature. The ironical mockery of it does not penetrate my fogbound consciousness.

I have a premonition that is undefined and which is over-shadowed by a cruder feeling that my sentence will end in death. But beneath both of these is an extremely delicate sense of something whose importance eludes me. This I know; I shall never weaken to the point where I beg like a dog for my release. I am equally sure that the deputy warden will hold fast to his promise. Not by the widest stretch of my imagination can I conceive that he would suddenly go soft, become chickenhearted, and weaken in his resolve to break my spirit and to make me whine for mercy. Such an event would throw him completely out of character. No, I feel doomed as I enter, a determined feeling that I am embracing a self-willed death, slow and paralysing, and indescribably painful.

The keeper of the "hole" is a stolid, thick-bellied, lumbering giant of a man, with a short, heavy neck, a massive, coarse face, and a closely-cropped, low-browed head. Set deeply in a pair of pouches are two small, piggish eyes, which remain dull even when his great hulking body is shaken with anger. To the convicts the keeper of "the hole" is known as "The Bull."

He takes an instant dislike to me, a sentiment which I return full measure, pressed down and running over. After I am stripped of my clothing he searches them. Then he turns his attention to my nude body, peers into my mouth, and examines me with frank suspicion, as he paws me with vulgar, ham-like hands, hoping to find some small instrument that could effect my escape, or suicide.

Defeated in this exploration, he gives me a thin, filthy blanket, a pair of unwashed cotton socks, an old pair of overalls, filled with the stench of their former victims, and a torn and faded shirt whose last wearer must have gone mad in a foaming fit, so stiff is the shirt's front.

Wearing these, I enter the dungeon. The Bull locks the steel door, and orders me to put my hands through the bars. I elevate them to a crossbar just above my head and obey his order, leaving an upright bar between my arms. The Bull clamps a pair of handcuffs around my wrists. With a parting curse he bangs shut the solid door. I begin my suicidal defiance of the deputy's iron will.

I know, of course, what this is going to mean. Each morning at six I am going to be chained up in this manner, after having been permitted to partake of a piece of bread and a cup of water. At six in the evening they will let me down for the night, when there will be another piece of bread and another cup of water. In the meantime, I shall have suffered the torments of suppressed bodily functions, or the loathsomeness of having had to exercise them.

I know that the maximum length of time for strong men in the cuffs is fifteen days; for the average, ten; and for the weakling, five. At the end of fifteen days the anus and legs are blue and swollen, the veins and arteries are enlarged and tight, while the bottoms of the feet are puffed and black with congealed blood. By this time the anus and legs are lifeless during the period in the cuffs. In its effort to pump blood into these dead members the heart becomes dangerously weakened. So the doctor will order me down at the end of the maximum sentence. Or so I think.

But this period comes and goes. I lose track of time. I hang my last day in the cuffs, for I have lost the power to stand. They lift me up to put me in them this morning. After this day—for many weeks after this—I just lie on the icy floor, emaciated and unspeakably filthy. They keep me alive with additional nourishment now. Death must not defeat the deputy's will. But I no longer feel hunger. To the cold I am inured, insensate. Each morning the deputy opens my solid door, pauses silently, tempting me to crawl to him and accede to his wishes. My only reaction is hatred for the man. I am now sustained by hate. The darkest curtain imaginable veils the future to the human consciousness.

THE FUTURE

How was I to know that the deputy warden would release me voluntarily? That he would permit the doctor to put me in the hospital from which I had planned to escape? How was I to know that even "The Bull" would become friendly, and the doctor alarmed about my condition? How was I to know that I would be trusted in one of the most responsible positions inside of prison walls, that of night nurse with its opportunity to traffic in all sorts of contraband, to say nothing of the opportunities it offered in aiding convicts to escape? How was I to know that one day I would be a respected member of society, honest and industrious? How was I to know that God's healing power would flow through me to others? That my prison doors would swing open five years in advance of the time set for my release? That a helpmate would be waiting outside for me ready to assist in the reconstruction of my broken life?

But I shall tell you how it all began.

WONDERMENT

A curious new thought eddied across my brain as I lay there with my hate and misery. Suddenly I became aware that all my life I had been a dynamo of energy. It had been years since I had entertained a constructive train of thought. Hence, this was a new and strange experience. It slipped up on me, so to speak, as a sense of wonderment. I began to wonder about my past life and what it would now be like if I had employed my energies and will power toward self-improvement and a genuine self-interest.

What followed is rather difficult to catch in the pattern of words. There were subtleties of feeling in it, elusive overtones too remote for external description. Adequately to apprehend such purely mystical sentiments one would have to experience them. I might describe the state as a gradual approach to that condition of consciousness wherein there seems to be a complete vacuum, a suspension of all volition.

The drift toward the state was characterized by a mild, dreamy sort of delirium in which I seemed to live half awake and half asleep.

That I was approaching what is commonly called mystical experience, I now know, but did not know at the time. At the point I have described as a vacuum, I was keenly aware of a revolutionary change taking place in my life. It was as though I were being reversed; or having been upside-down, was now being set a-right. For a long time I dwelt in an indescribable sense of awareness.

Then I began to dream in a confused and pointless way. Fragments of my life's experience, with neither beginning nor end, drifted mist-like across my mind. They seemed neither good nor bad—or at least my reactions to them were indifferent. This type of mental activity went on for several days and nights.

Finally and quite suddenly the form and content of these dreams changed. They now began to reveal consistency and continuity. They became rational and logical in form and sequence. Too, they were highly sane and beautiful in form and essence, filled with meaning and implied purpose. Then into my memory came the fact that I had known these dreams before—when I was a child. I became aware that I was dreaming of the man I had been trying to avoid for many years, Jesus the Christ.

The day came when he appeared to me as in a garden. And I remembered that this had been a childhood dream repeated in my subjective experience many times over. It was all so similar! His physical appearance, the quiet and vivid clarity of it, the thematic details, the rapturous feelings and the exalted thoughts it gave me! And now it seemed to be so purposeful!

He came toward me, his lips moving, but not vocally. He paused near my side and looked down, deep down into my eyes, as though through them he were trying to penetrate my soul. In all my life I had never seen or felt such love in the human eye as now glowed and radiated in his eyes. Nor had I ever felt myself so utterly helpless in the captivity of love. By some mysterious faculty of perception which operated in the midst of my dream, I seemed to know clearly that I was submerged in Reality; that I was seeing and feeling some-thing that would influence my life throughout all eternity.

The scene faded out casually, like some finger substance undergoing alteration, and becoming a formless mist which curled and drifted, even-tually forming itself into one word of gossamer, irregular letters. The word was LOVE. *This, too, vanished, leaving me for what seemed an age enveloped in an unspeakable state of mental clarity. As I had previously felt myself receiving love, I now had the joyous sense of bestowing love. It poured from me in gratitude and blissful tears. I loved all men. I hated only the evil conditions they imposed upon each other and upon them-selves. I loved the world. I loved God. Then I dreamed again.*

Once more the form of the dream was like a scroll or a motion picture film being unwound. There was no pain in it this time; it was all elation, ecstasy. All the people I had injured directly and indirectly came before me again and this time I gave them love, which seemed to soothe and heal their hurts. Then all the people who had injured me appeared. One by one I began to help them and love them. It was all exceedingly vivid. Out of the scroll a great auditorium took form. There was a huge audience. They were all the people I had injured and who had injured me. I spoke to them con-cerning love as one who had the right to speak with authority. I was aware that my diction was positively flawless, my enunciation matchless. So vivid was this, I found myself entertaining a parallel train of thought in which I seemed to be assuring myself that I was not dreaming, that I was surely awake, and that I would never forget these words which were flowing over my lips in such incomparable cadences of love and conviction.

Thus, as a recipient of love, I became a transmitter of it. It seemed to rise from within me and flow outward, as though generated from some interior source. The joy and bliss and gratitude I felt was past articulation, and was wholly uncontainable. In the midst of such feeling I knew I must either be changed or I would die.

I was grateful not for any particular thing, but for all good, for life itself. I had no discernment apart from this nameless clarity of thought and perception, this boundless enchantment of universal love and reality. I knew that I had transcended all personal and bodily limitations of habit and environment that had bound me through the years. I had no sense of my prison walls, but my thoughts roamed the imponderable Universe far and clear. The measurements of Time and Space vanished out of my consciousness. I was free. I knew I was free. I had found the Reality within the actuality, the breath within the breath, the consciousness within the consciousness, the soul within the form. And above all, I knew that I was being what the theologians call "reborn."

To this day I am not positively certain as to why this experience became a new and different chapter in the book of my life. Nor am I sure as to just how it was brought about. A few men and women who claim knowledge of such things have told me that it was due to my mother's pronounced religious impulse, which was also harboured secretly by my father. This, they claim, was inherited by me. The intense outer conflict with the forces of law and order had acted to compress my true character until, in a state of physical, emotional, and mental exhaustion, a rock-bottom crisis was reached, those finer energies were released, and the soul burst through the weakened barriers and swept upward and onward into a new order of expression.

If this be so, if the self-willed suffering of my life had anything to do with it, I can only say that I did not suffer in vain. For a single second in which Reality is known is worth a lifetime of misery.

I do not propose, however, to offer an explanation of the experience. If an explanation or defence were needed I feel now, as I have always felt, that it would have been given me at the time.

I am intensely interested in superphysical experience as an experientialist. I have read quite widely on the subject from the works of those who have themselves passed this way. This range of reading has given me much information of a biographical nature. It has shown me an assortment of widely different personalities and temperaments, who for an instant found the veil removed from ordinary vision, permitting them to catch a glimpse of the wider world and a more distant horizon. Possessing the literary gift, they have been able to relate their experiences with some measure of accuracy, but as to *why* and *how* they join the union of silence.

William James in his *Varieties of Religious Experience* attempts the psychological explanation of such experiences in others. But of his own Adirondack experience his explanation is pitifully inadequate. Here he admits that he did not know what it was or why it was. He is content to refer to it briefly and without meaning as "a boulder of impression."

In my prologue I have put down other psychological explanations. *Apparently that which is superconscious transcends and thus defies the ordinary processes of conscious transmission.*

When I consciously returned to my dungeon environment the state of my mind was no longer the same. It had power to give me joy but not pain. The cell was illumined with a new kind of light, the light of my own redeemed eye. It was the same dark, cold place; but now it was warm and congenial. It became the reflector of my glowing inner self. My imagination was exceptionally keen. I began to experiment with it immediately. I decorated the barren damp walls with things of beauty and quality. I appointed the cell with a fireplace and a mantel, with rugs and tables and deep chairs. When I had finished I had done the job well. The colour scheme was harmonious and the placements correct. Everything was in good taste.

Next I invited guests. I still wonder if they were mere figments of my imagination. They were always the same. I willed it, and they appeared. Did I imagine them or did they take advantage of an opportunity I offered? Can any great literary genius affirm that the powerful characters moving through his pages are his creations? My characters were men, each a composite figure in his own orbit. They all moved in an aura of allegory. They stood for Love, Wisdom and Faith. Taking their seats before my imaginary fire they would engage in a sort of exalted symposium, quite oblivious of me sitting in the foreground, a one-man audience. The things they discussed are etched upon my memory today—things that would no doubt tax the reader's credulity, but that have never ceased to act as a beneficial influence in my life.

In this experience my old fears vanished, but a new one, which was born out of the experience, appeared. This was the fear that I would be released from the dungeon, and thus, perhaps, in different surroundings, might become divorced from my joy and serenity. I greatly preferred to remain apart, hugging to myself the raptures of my newly-found freedom. I was, however, protected even from this elevated temptation, this exalted suicide, which inevitably leads to selfishness and in the end to spiritual bankruptcy. Jesus had turned away from this course, preferring to share rather than to clutch to himself the heavenly estate.

Before this experience I was an ingrained and calloused criminal. After it I was as completely healed of my criminal tendencies as anyone could be healed. Too, this healing has given me a certain reach and practical utility, the like of which I could not have attained otherwise.

The experience left me with an energy which is felt as a sense of assurance and ability. It may be more precisely called *faith*, the common meaning of which Professor Glenn Clark describes in his *Fishers of Men*, and which weaves like a strong thread through his finer work, *The Soul's Sincere Desire*. In reading these volumes one has a definite sense of faith as a practical as well as a spiritual energy, which is applicable even in the training of athletes—an energy that can be consciously applied to business, trade, profession, and in fact, to any practical and needful services of the world.

To cite an example of the application of this energy: At the time of the experience, while not entirely illiterate, I was, nevertheless, inarticulate from the standpoint of ordinary education. I could read cheap literature after a fashion, and I could manage a legible note or brief letter.

Following the experience, I was strongly drawn to the parables of Jesus and whatever jokes I could secure from Lincoln. For in these latter I seemed to perceive the content of the parable. In other words, out of my experience I was left with a curious but persistent interest in parabolic writings.

Two parables of Jesus in particular interested me, "The Prodigal Son," and "The Parable Of The Vine." After reading the former a number of times, I felt the vastness of its theme and the matchless perfection of its literary quality. I seemed almost impelled to write a short story after the manner of this parable. What is more, despite my limitations, I felt that I could do it.

Finally, annoyed by the urge, I secured some wrapping paper and began the task. I named my story, "There's Another Law," which dealt with the theme of retribution. The finished story missed the pattern of the parable by a million miles, but I got permission to send it outside to a friend, who in turn sent it to *Detective Story.* The editor liked it, bought it, and wrote me a letter asking for more. I was elated over this bit of success and decided thereupon to make a career of story writing. Later I obtained a correspondence course in the art, studied it diligently, and began to bombard my friendly editor. All my other efforts missed the mark. They came back with an unbroken regularity. I might have done better if I had remained true to my first model.

THE MIRACLE WORKER

There was in my experience an instant, which for want of a better name, I have called a vacuum. The actual miracle of healing happened in this instant. What went before was but a prologue. What followed was but an epilogue. The miracle-working power was love. Of that I am convinced. Of its mystery I know less as I learn more. Through the years that have followed the evidence has piled up. There is miracle magic in love. I do not know what love is. I gather examples of its workability. I know it has a practical utility, as well as a spiritual glory. I know it never fails to change the thing it touches. Out of disorder it brings order, out of chaos harmony. The examples of this crowd my life and the files of my personal mail. No revelations as to what love is come through, save that it is Reality, that it is greater than man's power to define. It fills all space, and without it nothing could survive, no planet could wheel, no insect flit, no plant grow—nothing could be born, and nothing could be reborn, except for the miracle work of love.

I have learned something of its ways. This for instance: The miracles wrought by love power are seldom obvious. Love works quietly, like an artist at his task, an inventor at his bench, a scientist in his den of wonders. There are many major similarities between love and science, love and art, love and invention. Science, art, and invention are content to do the thing, to act and to let the result happen. Too, they allow their fruits to preach for them. In the heart of an artist, scientist, inventor there is little desire to reform the world or anybody in it. Their motive is to achieve. This is their drive. If this is done the world will benefit.

But there is a major difference. The fruits of science, art, and invention *can* be turned against humanity. Love heals the wound it does not make. There is a selfish emotion that hurts. It has often been called love. It is but the shadow of the miracle worker.

Just as science, art, and invention do not desire to reform anybody, neither does love. By not wanting to reform others it transforms them. By setting others free, love binds them. A friend is a lover. He does not preach, find fault, condemn. He frees; and the thing he frees he binds. You cannot have the thing you will not give away. You cannot be free of the thing you hold. To hold on is to belong to the thing held, a *bond*. What you set free belongs to you. You do not belong to it, for you belong to love. To be in bondage to love—this is the needful thing, for then all good belongs to you. To belong to less than love is to be the slave and not the master. To belong to love is to have life and life abundantly, for then life belongs to you. To belong to life is to be in bondage to Time and Space. All things below love encircle and squeeze. They press and inflict and hurt. Love is Reality, the liberator, the miracle worker. By making others glad, love brings them the foretaste of heaven on earth.

Jesus knew the great miracle-working secret. He didn't preach to the multitudes. He went about telling stories and loving people. Simply by loving them he healed them. His love excited their love, and in love they were set free, their lives changed. Always this happens where the wellsprings of love are unloosed. *No one with love ever fails. No one without it ever succeeds. Love does not force a thing to happen. It lets the thing happen.* The next thing is always the best thing for the compassionate. A forced success puts one in bondage to work. The end is tension and boredom. One must maintain by force that which is born out of time by force. The lover plays at his task. No motion is lost. He achieves more in an hour than the forcer achieves in a day. The latter is bound by his achievement. In his achievement the former is set free.

Our files are filled with voluntary testimonies; to our living room they come as verbal witnesses. A woman told of her ruined home. Her husband drank and gambled. The psychologists, she said, went limp before her problem. Her pastor fidgeted, glanced often at his watch, and quoted Jesus.

It was a tragic story, a stimulation to love. Her sixteen-year-old daughter laughed at her good advice and accused her of habitual nagging. Her nineteen-year-old son affected a condescending air of tolerance towards her and drifted on in the footsteps of his father. She filled her weekly engagements before the women's clubs, speaking on domestic science and child psychology.

"I'm well equipped," she said, giving a thumbnail history of her academic background. "And God knows I've tried hard enough to change them," she added hopelessly, "but I've failed. They resist everything I say and do."

There was a pause. Into it we dropped a seed. *"Love is not trying. It is ceasing to try."*

"I do love them," she affirmed. "But maybe not in the right way. I don't know how to love any differently."

"Are you willing to admit failure, that you can do nothing about it?" we asked.

She nodded wearily, genuinely contrite, humble.

"Then you're in the most powerful position in all the world," we told her. A new hope came to her sad eyes and grew as we talked. "All you have to do is to stop trying to change them. Turn them over to God with a confession that you're helpless in the matter. And turn yourself over with them. Tell Him that you have given them back to Him with no strings attached, and with no compromises or bargains. Tell Him frankly and honestly that you don't care what He does with them, if anything, or when or how He does it. Tell Him they are His. That you're completely free of them. But then add that you will do, to the best of your ability the two things He has given you power to do in the matter: *you will love them without self-seeking and without possessiveness, and you will do every direct and indirect thing you can as a contribution to their happiness."*

Even as we talked, invisible fingers went to work in her household. Nearly every day she had a new report to make over the phone. All of a sudden her husband began to display his old acts of thoughtfulness and considerateness towards her. His old interest in the home was renewed. His interest in the tavern and the pinball machines and the dice tables vanished. Her daughter began to seek her for counsel, to confide her adolescent problems, and to share in the household duties as though she loved to do it. Her son's superficial air of tolerance towards her changed to one of genuine affection. Finally she wrote from a mountain resort, where they had all gone for a family vacation. The letter closed with the following sentences: "You wrote about the Seattle woman as the happiest woman in the world. If she is any happier than I am, then she is in heaven. That is all I have to say."

Do I know the mystery of love, the liberator, the life-giver, the joy-maker? No. I know of its fruits. For the present I am content with this. To ponder love philosophically is fascinating, no doubt. But I'd rather see it work, actually. My friends, who like to speculate upon abstract theories, may smile at this, but it is as far as I've gone. The philosophical "why" of love may come later. In the meantime I'll continue to gather evidence and pass out reports.

There is surely miracle magic in love. And love does things so naturally and simply. You have to pause and think about it before you can see the miracle in the result, so well does love hide its handiwork. It is rarely sensational, obviously phenomenal, spectacular. Love just laughs and plays at the game of life. Where love is, work is play, and play is always creative work. Wherever love caresses, confusion and disorder vanish, boredom, the great vice, melts, inertia dies, disharmony is swallowed up, old fears fade out, old wounds are healed, leaving no scar tissue, resentments and grudges are impossible, cheap gossip and tawdry fault-finding disappear: joy and health are established, life becomes gladness, optimism and goodwill, the sufferings of others are shared and released. Love gives freedom to all without in the slightest degree allowing freedom to be twisted into licence.

Love never plucks a soul prematurely. It is content to aid the ripening process and do the plucking in time and season. Nor does it force the ripening with undue persuasion or play upon fearful emotions concerning the wraths and judgments of God. Love knows that God is tender and merciful, that man is judged by his own judgment, condemned by his own condemnation, impoverished by his own greed and mass selfishness. Love waits for man to come to himself, to weary of his self-willed futility, arrogance and suffering, to tire of the darkness that condemns himself and generations yet unborn. Love knows and waits for opportunities to act. No opportunity is offered which love does not seize. It reaches twice as far as man is willing to reach. The creature's failure is love's chance.

It was so in my case.

Nor does love ever seek to amend itself with reason, logic, common sense. Love is the supreme reason, the matchless logic, the robust common sense. Love makes the ordinary things extraordinary, the common things uncommon, the weak things strong, the little things huge, the low things high.

Love knows that like attracts like, that love excites love, and that to love the neighbour is to excite one's love for God. "To love is always to know; but to know is not always to love." The love that knows is spiritual. The other love is intellectual. In the former love redemption is present, release for the soul. The latter love has light without warmth. Spiritual love is the sun, both light and warmth. Intellectual love is the moon, a reflector of light, but not a generator of heat. Spiritual love is the Son of God. Intellectual love is the son of man, who has not yet dreamed what manner of man he is to be. Spiritual love is Christ-centric. Intellectual love is egocentric.

Intellectual love, therefore, cannot equal the power in spiritual love. But by the persistent and purposeful practice of intellectual love, spiritual love can be excited. At the point where the *love thought fuses* with the *love feeling* the miracle happens, healing takes place, order appears, the soul unfolds her wings.

Hence the needful thing is to love. There is no prison door visible or invisible, which love cannot open, no prison stripe which love cannot melt. There is no fear or worry which love cannot use to good advantage, not by forcing the fear out, but by transforming into lifting power the energy which fear and worry generate.

What, then, happens when the force of sin meets the power of compassion? Both the sinner and the compassionate are lifted up to the heavenly consciousness. "I am kept in heaven by the energy of sin," said a saintly man to me one day. With bright, twinkling eyes, a glow of gratitude upon his face, he explained the process:

"The Lord sends the sinners to me. I sit down with them and do nothing but love them and listen to their troubles. They are filled with negative energy, which they pour out to me. My love for them transforms that energy as fast as they release it. Pretty soon they are empty. A peace has come. Because of their trouble we have both found heaven on earth. Being in heaven they are healed, and I am blest. We have served each other: the sinner serving most."

Oh, yes, there is miracle magic in the power of love.

THE INNER RADIANCE

Light and Love, the mind and the heart of God. Within every man the light shineth, though it be in darkness. God delays for man but He does not desert him. And "God is Light." So proclaims the Scriptures: "This then is the message which we have heard of Him, and declare unto you, that God is Light." (1 John 1:5.)

In the darkness, both of my life and environment, I found that inner light that discovers God to man. This light dwells within every human being and is separated from the darkness, which is also within him. It says to the darkness, "Thus far and no farther." In a lighted house we have an illustration of the eternal separation of the light and the dark. When the light comes in, the dark goes out, and when the dark comes in, the light goes out. The two cannot abide in the same place at the same time. The dark fears and hates the light, as evil fears and hates the good.

Locked up in the tissues of man's brain and nervous system is this inner light the brightness of which completely swallows up the ordinary light of his intelligence. Many, by seeking the inner radiance, have found it. Once it has been loosed in a man he can never be the same. Thereafter he must give himself to it or suffer.

This inner light is the light of the awakened soul. Once awake she will never rest or sleep again until she has attained her complete emancipation. There is no suffering to equal that of the man who, having experienced the soul's radiance, denies her dream of permanent releasement, and who refuses to cooperate with her toward the realization of that dream. Having been bathed in her light once, a man must either change or die a thousand deaths daily.

Upon some the inner light has burst like a flash in the night, unsought and unexpected. This was the experience of the Apostle Paul. His soul had long been betrayed by the darkness of his keen brain. Bent upon a dark mission, he was stopped short in his tracks, the inner light broke, and he was caught up in the white radiance of an unspeakable Reality. He either had to change or perish. He changed. He was translated in a second of mortal time. Now walking himself in the light he could write to his followers: "Ye were once in the darkness, but are now light in the Lord. Walk as children of light."

A man who has been given the advantages of education is like a lighted candle. The candle itself is the organic, physical man. The flame is the carnal mind, the light of human intelligence. But within that outer light, which flickers and is streaked with yellow murkiness, there can be seen, if closely observed, an inner light, clear and white and steady. This is God's inner radiance in man, the light of the soul.

There are many ways whereby the inner light may be set free. Spiritual meditation releases it, and prayer. A steady day by day self-discipline in goodness and mercy brings a glow, a lustre to the face of the spiritual workman. Seeing in the little things opportunities for the big things has a way of wooing the inner spark outward. To put one hand in the hand of Christ and the other in the hand of a brother—this is the Royal Way of Him who could say, "I am the light of the world: he that followeth me shall not walk in darkness, but shall have the light of life."

There is the way of the *imitation of Christ* and the way of *practising the presence of God*. For every person there is a way to the WAY about whom the gospel writer reported, "In him was life, and the life was the light of men," and about whom He Himself reported, "I am the way, the truth, and the life." He is the mountain top experience. He is the Final Way. There are ways and ways and ways winding up the mountainside to Him. Of these innumerable ways many are curious and strange.

Experience has taught me to respect them all, to cast a pious sneer at none.

Years ago I was employed in a prison knitting factory. My wages? The wages of sin, a living death. Our daily task was heavy, and to most of us the working hours were long. There was one man in our shop, however, who seemed not to mind the pressure of time and the tear of toil. His work was always well done, and his daily task was usually finished and turned in a couple hours in advance of any one else. I was destined one day to discover and use his secret.

We called him Easy-Going Slim, because of his even disposition. He possessed that rare quality of meekness, which was anything but weakness. After a man has served ten years in prison he is likely to develop odd mannerisms and eccentric habits, a mild sort of insanity. Thereafter, in the prison vernacular, he becomes known as a "stir bug." Easy-Going Slim had been so dubbed. At this time he had spent thirteen of his best years behind prison walls.

A newcomer to prison, who had not yet been informed, mistook Slim's lamb-like manner for cowardice one day. He made a slurring remark about one of Slim's habitual oddities. The lean and lengthy old-timer turned to his traducer. He showed no more emotion than a cud-chewing cow. He spoke as one making a quiet confession. It was a prelude to action:

"The Master'd overlook that," he said to the unwise prison recruit. "But I ain't the Master. Wish I was. I'd agree with ya quickly. An' fergive ya, if I was. Maybe some day I'll be man a-nuff to hear ya and turn the other ear fer the other barrel. But in the meantime—" A swift blow to the other fellow's jaw replaced the end of the sentence.

Ten days later they both returned from solitary confinement to resume their task, the one a wiser and less hasty man, the other to take up the odd habit, which the incident had interrupted.

Each afternoon, at the conclusion of his daily task, Easy-Going Slim would go to a line in the concrete floor that ran the full length of the shop. With deliberate and studied leisureliness he would walk this line, back and forth until quitting time, completely absorbed in the action, wholly unconcerned about the opinions of others who held the habit up to silent ridicule. As far as the rest of us were concerned it was just another eccentric way invented by the "stir bug" to overcome monotony and kill time.

Actually, however, it was a way invented by Slim to practise the Royal Way of Jesus—that Royal Way of the straight and narrow path. *This daily walking of the straight and narrow line, with a purpose, was not only an effective physical discipline, but was a constant reminder to think straight and live straight,* if he was ever to break the crooked spell that had held him for a lifetime in the bondage of crime and useless suffering.

I met Easy-Going Slim a few years ago. He was vacationing on the West Coast with his wife and two children. At fifty-five he looked younger than he did as a convict at thirty-five. His old prison pallor had long ago been displaced by a spiritual lustre. There was a bright twinkle of perpetual joy in his eye, instead of the old furtive glint and dull cast of frustration. He now possessed no drag to the left leg, nor was his language of the old prison variety, "I seen my duty and done it." His vocabulary was rich with simple words, which he used correctly. His work was advertising, but his subject was Christ, and Him the way of life.

His way to the WAY had been a curious one. But it had gotten him there. By it he had found and released the inner light, which was to set him free, and by which he could walk straight, now erect and fearless, now life-glad and honest. I could have, had I so desired, sat in cold, self-righteous judgment of his means. Of his ends, however, I could have offered no critical comment.

I recall another prisoner who found his way into the place of inner radiance. His way, too, caused him to be dubbed a *freak*, a *crack-pot*, a *stir bug*, by his slap-happy, prison-wise fellows. I was among them. But in his case I did wake up to the thought that, queer though his practice was, there might be something behind it after all.

Because of his strange conduct we called him Pitty-Pat.

Once when he was in the prison hospital convalescing from an illness, he would sometimes sit for two or three hours at a time, his back as straight as a stove poker, his legs straight out before him, feet firmly on the floor, palms pressed over his knees, eyes closed. In this position he would lift up his toes. Up would raise the fingers at the same time. Then down again would go the toes and the fingers. Up and down, up and down, up and down. Time seemed to mean nothing, the pitty-patting everything to him.

I was employed as a night nurse in the hospital at the time. One afternoon I enquired sympathetically into the meaning of Pitty-Pat's peculiar behaviour.

"You're intelligent," he replied. "You're the only bird in this cage who's ever asked that with any sense. I'll tip you off to something," he added, lowering his voice to a confidential tone.

It turned out to be a system for meditation. Pitty-Pat called it the practice of a *tedium*. He explained that if you held your personal will on a thing that was tedious enough, and you held your will on it long enough, your will would finally get weary of the monotony and give up.

"Where our own will ends," he said, "God's will begins. The trouble with people in this world is self-will. They think they can find the light by running to and fro in the earth. People are like monkeys. They can't keep still. They think they've got to chatter all the time. No wonder they can't find God."

My interest brought forth additional information. Pitty-Pat explained that the breath we breathed was oxygen. But in a higher sense it was spirit. As proof of this assertion he referred me to the

Book of Genesis and to the passage where the Lord God breathed the breath of life into a lifeless form made of dust and the form became a living soul.

"That breath of life," said Pitty-Pat, "was oxygen. That's what the body needs to live on. But the life of the soul is spirit. So every time we breathe we bring spirit to the soul as well as oxygen to the body. Now just watch," he went on, "and you'll get next to something great."

He put his feet and hands in order. "I breathe in as my toes and hands come up," he said, as he performed the action. "While the breath is coming in, I tell myself mentally that this breath is spirit. My toes and hands go down as I breathe out. And I tell myself mentally that I breathe out love. Don't tell anyone I've told you about this. They'll scoff at it. You don't toss sacred things to dogs. And you don't cast pearls before swine," he finished solemnly.

Pitty-Pat's method for seeking, and finding, the light within would set the tongues of some present-day psychologists to wagging. They would probably accuse him of self-hypnosis, or of deliberately inducing a trance state in order to produce a luminous experience. But Pitty-Pat, a thoroughly conditioned criminal, healed himself by his curious, eccentric method. Before that healing the dreariest cynic and most envious critic must take a back seat and fall silent. What the prisoner actually did was to produce in his consciousness a condition of passivity, or stillness. It did not make an ascetic or a useless hermit of him. It made a man of him, a very positive and capable man, who has taken his place in society as a servant instead of an enemy. He no longer follows the *way*. He has now taken his place on the WAY itself, the Royal Way behind the Royal WAY-SHOWER.

The mystical experience is not an uncommon thing in the prison life, though few ever become sufficiently articulate later to report it.

I knew a boy to be caught up in the light during my first prison stretch. I didn't understand it at the time. When he tried to tell me what had happened I laughed at him. He was lying on the bunk above me. He had received a letter from his mother that evening. After he had read it he had been uncommonly still for a long time, staring at the wall beyond his feet. He dozed off with the letter held in his hand over his breast. Suddenly he woke with a start, his face illumined. He said he had dreamed he could see his mother down on her knees praying for him. *Then suddenly he thought he had turned into a blaze of pure white light. The youngster was never the same afterwards.* He was very sensitive to sin, and when his sentence ended his prison experience was never to be repeated.

Another old offender, who had grown weary with prison life, arranged to have himself put into the cell with a fellow who was known to be a fanatic on religion. By making himself agree with this man's religious convictions he came into a radiant spiritual experience a year later which changed his whole life, attitude, and behaviour.

A most remarkable example of *illumination* was related to me recently by the man himself. For a couple of years I had been in correspondence with him while he served time in prison, his fourth major conviction.

He admitted to me that in the beginning his motives were *rank*. He had figured out that I might have a little influence outside that he could use, and that if he couched his letters in just the right accents, I might send him a few dollars from time to time. This motive I picked up easily, partly by knowledge gained through my own underworld experience, and also by intuition. I reply only to about one out of twenty letters reaching me from the prisons. My work with prisoners has been neither extensive nor conspicuous. It has dealt with individuals. With them it has been successful. But where I have tried to deal with groups by means of a form or group letter the effort has been uniformly unsuccessful.

In spite of his unwholesome motives, however, I replied to this man's opening. His letters grew rich and vital as the months passed, and they contained much fresh information, which I could pass on through the printed page.

In this kind of ministry one never knows what one is going to put into a letter. It is a reply the material of which is a response to the other's promptings. One never knows when a phrase or a sentence will become as a seed dropped in fertile soil, or as a spark dropped into a box of ready tinder. In one of my letters I quoted an old and timeworn Egyptian truism, "As below so above." This was the beginning of an ethical adventure that was to end in a flash of inner light and in the redemption of a human personality.

The phrase intrigued the man. It stuck in his mind. He wrestled with it and finally began to ponder it and to seek evidence for its support. This evidence began to accumulate, until in time he felt justified in assuming that the statement was true. He began to act upon this assumption.

In the underworld, where he had spent most of his life, he had, among other things, been a professional gambler. He had accepted the gambler's philosophy that life was a game of chance, a gamble from the cradle to the grave, and that the percentage was always on the side of the dealer.

Life had discovered for him, however, that in the world even the professional gambler with the percentage in his favour always lost in the long run, for even to win the stake was to be punished by it. He who dealt in the vice-rimmed game below had his winnings recorded as losses in the tablet of virtue above. But it came to dawn upon him that there was one Dealer in the game of life who had all the percentage on His side, who never lost a bet either in the short or long run. It then occurred to him that if the professional gambler had one brain cell throbbing in tune with wisdom, he would place himself on the side of that Dealer.

He decided there and then to do his gambling for God.

He first staked his prisoner reputation and prestige as a loyal comrade of the underworld against the withering ostracism of his fellow convicts for those who weaken and *go religious*. But if God was the Dealer, and he was on the Dealer's side of the table, the percentage was with him, and in the end he would win.

Openly he declared himself. Openly he began to carry his cell Bible with him, and keep it open before him as he performed his work. He was learning the game of life according to God's rules of the game. As he learned he began to play for high stakes, the ripe and ready souls of others. He found himself winning souls before his own was won.

One day a peculiar sensitivity occurred in his consciousness. A youth, half-silly from self-abuse and prison punishment, warped and twisted and degraded in the losing game of life, withdrew to a corner in the shop. He pushed back from his own machine, went up to the youth and said, "Slip me that knife." It was like hearing someone speaking through his own lips. He himself had not the slightest idea that the boy possessed a knife.

The youth looked at him, fear in his eyes. "How'd you know I had it?" he asked.

"Never mind, slip it to me." Then he heard himself saying: "You were going to knife this warder. Don't you do it. You'll roast for it if you do."

The youth gave him the knife, and with it an invitation into his private and innermost life. One day he led that boy straight to God. And that night in his cell he bowed his head to offer up thanks for this display of God's grace and mercy, and while in this attitude an unearthly light burst from his own soul, which for a glorious, bliss-filled moment ravished him in the arms of Reality.

From that day on the game became more exciting. The thrill, the fever and excitement of the play steadily mounted, until the thrill, the fever and excitement of the old smoke-dense gambling room had been completely eclipsed in his blood. To him gambling for God had become the most life-thrilling game in the world.

What a thrill it was to step out boldly on faith and cease the struggle. How exciting it was to aim at a goal and then rest on God for guidance to reach it. With sympathetic understanding he could now marvel at the sweat, blood, and tears people shed to compel their objectives, only to find in the achievement a sour taste, a satiation, a bondage, a drag.

This man is now engaged in helping others to the light that he himself found. He tells of the light within that can banish the darkness of sin and worry and strife. He points out the importance of starting the day with the realization that the percentage is on the side of God and that you are where the percentage is. He tells how effective it is to begin all important undertakings with spiritual preparation, and to keep the high noon communion, the evening recollection of God's blessings and silence. He points out the importance of keeping still within even in the throes of the noisy, workaday world, for it is in this silence that God speaks to man; it is here that the light bursts; it is into this vacuum that the stream of living water flows.

CHAPTER 7

THE AFTER RADIANCE

THERE IS A GREAT DIFFERENCE BETWEEN A CRIMINAL WHO HAS been reformed by man's methods and one who has been transformed by God's grace and power. The former may never be wholly trusted and may relapse at any time under disappointment and temptation. No pressure can force or no temptation can lure the latter into the criminal fold as a repeater of offence. His temptations may be and usually are far more numerous and compelling, but if he has been genuinely regenerated and not merely stirred up emotionally, he will bear with fortitude the most exacting demands which life can make upon his newly acquired way of living. *And if these seem more than he can reasonably bear, he will have an immovable sense of protection and victory to aid him. There will be an Invisible Hand to snatch him back from the brink—a Guardian Angel to watch over him!*

I returned to the round of prison life glowing with a huge zeal, imbued with an inner radiance. My overpowering desire to share these graces with my fellows caused me to ignore discrimination and to cast my gems with a lavish hand before the unready and unripened souls with whom I immediately came in contact. This lack of discernment got me into difficulty on every hand. I took it for granted that everyone would want what I had received, and I felt as though I *must* work fast. I was to discover that the Lord has no more use for busybodies than has man. The troubles piled upon me fast and thick.

My main difficulty was no longer with the prison officials. To them I did not have to proclaim my healing. The changed life proclaimed itself. My fellow convicts also recognized the change in me.

However, instead of this proving attractive to them it proved in many instances extremely repulsive. They preferred to resent and reject the altered man. My old bitter, sour pals, especially, refused the new model. They spoke in sarcastic accents of me. They referred to me as "the tough guy who had weakened in the hole, and had turned yellow in the cuffs."

Nearly all my life I had preached the gospel of hate. In prison I had been associated with those who preached a like gospel. As I had been suspicious of those who "got religion," so were they doubly suspicious of me now that I had fallen under the spell. A short while before I had been in sympathy and accord with all the prison rebels. Now I was facing them as one out of sympathy, as one no longer friendly to the cause of crime and protest. I was a man with a new preachment on my lips. The ears which had long been in tune with my old hymns of hate found my new hymns far too much on the side of the upper world and too little in harmony with the underworld.

Had my experience happened while I was in the outside world, the adjustment would have been comparatively easy. Then I could have chosen a corresponding company, and I could have avoided those who sneered at me. But here I was hedged in by high walls. Those who had been my friends had become my enemies. I was compelled to face them as such and to be made to hear and feel their withering remarks; to stand accused in their eyes as one who had sold out and gone over to the official camp, perhaps as a stool pigeon in search of tainted favours. Ostracism is hard to bear in the penitentiary, and every convict courts it who makes a deliberate bid for official popularity.

I had been popular with the convict body before my experience. Now, after the experience and without deliberate effort, I was popular with the official body. There were days as lonely as those which Benedict Arnold must have lived; days in which I was painfully conscious of bearing the mark of the traitor. I had to possess the strong reinforcements of the Spirit to journey through these valleys and come out with my new faith unbroken. The changed life, if it be genuine, will stand severe testing. It will be shaken to its foundation but the supports will hold. *Both strength to bear and light to overcome will be given in the hour when the personal resources fail—so it proved in my case.*

Since I could not escape the barbs of my enemies, I was given direction and power to overcome them. My desire was to live this newly discovered life and to share it with others. This, then, was my direction and my power that I was to have no choice apart from Christ's commandment to love my enemies. My indiscriminate and zealous methods having failed, there remained the quiet method of patience and indirection.

I learned to convert my enemies into objects for practice and self-improvement. To return my love for my enemy's hate was one of the great teachings of Jesus by which I could practise the presence of God. With this leading, the desire to change my old friends faded as a motivating force in my life. To accept them as a means of strengthening my own position became the impelling motive behind my action.

To this end I began to fashion a mental portrait gallery of all my enemies. During the day and night I would take them in turn, bring them before my mind's eye, and identify them with me in terms of love and a true and noble friendship. This practice made a highly fascinating game of life. It was filled with surprises, sudden and unexpected reversals of those who had been avoiding me, little miracles they were which greatly enriched my faith and added steel to my unfolding character.

However uncomplimentary it may be from a spiritual point of view, I did receive a very warm, personal satisfaction in seeing the conscious application of love work these miracles in the lives of my avowed enemies, as well as in my own life; of sitting quietly on the side-line watching old barriers melt away and old friendships being re-established upon a new and nobler basis. To me this was one of the most mysterious, profound, and beautiful things I had yet discovered about the transforming power of love: that it could be deliberately and consciously applied to specific cases and problems. I learned by experiment and experience that love could be directed, that it could reach and affect the dreariest outcast and melt the stone casing around the most unregenerate heart. Here was the grace of God available to the toughest enemy of Christ and man. That it could be distributed through me, brought an undisguised sense of joy out of my soul.

But on the other hand, mighty questions arose in my mind—questions which down the ages have disturbed the thinkers, the advance guards of the race, and which these thinkers have tried vainly to answer. If love could change a man as it had me and as I had seen it change enemies into friends, why was it not more generally used by an organized society, crime-ridden and war afflicted, sick unto death with failure and suffering?

During my many years in prison no less than a dozen prison chaplains had tried earnestly but in vain to guide my feet through the door of Christ and out into the lush green pastures of a glad, new life. But equipped though they were with Christ's gospel they had not succeeded. It remained for a fellow convict, a simple old lifer, to clarify the teachings of Jesus for me and so to interpret them as to make God real and close and knowable. But why had the chaplains failed? Had they somehow failed in themselves to take hold of love and direct its recreative power toward the objects of their interest? Had they failed to employ the power of love in their ministry? If so, why?

There were questions of ethics and theology. Why did Paul continue the example of creeds, which had sapped the vitality from all other systems of religion, and had left them dying or dead in the midst of their endless outer observances, their days and seasons, their pomps and displays? I had to go beyond, always beyond first reactions to the conflicting units of organized Christianity, and to see even in these a healthy sign for the endurance of Christ and his matchless leadership. The very squabbles between the creeds were evidence of Christ's vitality and versatility. His most vociferous enemies and robust antagonists declared his unavoidable reality with every blast of denial. There was no way to escape Christ. Whether for or against him, he was advertised. Those who would continue to destroy him could succeed only in promoting interest in him.

There were those who could answer my questions concerning the mysteries and contradictions upon a basis of Bible authority, but not upon personal experience. And I would ask "why," and then "why."

As I look back now it seems to me that these chaplains had a love in their hearts for us. But I wonder if it was sufficient. Perhaps it was divided by certain unconscious prejudices built up through the centuries by social attitudes. Perhaps it was too much modified by unconscious personal opinion. Perhaps it was depleted by too much theological learning. Perhaps the old lifer who could help me had less to unlearn than our chaplains. Being on my own social level, his might have been a more advantageous position. However, one convict is not prone to take pious advice from another unless that other actually lives his doctrine.

This old lifer had many key passages out of the Gospels, which he believed and lived with every cell in his body and with every impulse of his mind and heart. He took, for example, the following passage to mean just what it said: "By this shall all men know that ye are my disciples, if ye have love one to another." (John 13:35.)

Early in our friendship he told me that the greatest service one man could render to another was to love him without strings and without indulging his weaknesses. For he said to love a man was to understand him, and to understand him was to be able to help him and heal him—thus God, the healing power, was made available to him through love.

"Love never faileth," he would quote. "Love casts out fear." "Love is the fulfilling of the law." "God is love." "Every man that loveth is born of God, and knoweth God." And then he would say: "The test of your religion is not knowledge or wisdom. A hate-filled atheist may possess either. It is not faith or creed. The Devil himself has faith and an unbending creed. It is not healing or interpretation. The worst sinner can heal and a man with no control over his own animal nature can interpret. It is not the capacity to discern spirits and perform miracles. The unregenerate may do both. The final test of your religion is a love-filled heart. The love of God and the love of man."

He once put it this way to me: "Your love of God is His love of you in action. As your love goes out to man in a Godlike way it is His love expressing itself through you. You are with God when you express His love. You have but one obligation in the world, to let God's love transform your love."

I believe this old lifer knew whereof he spoke, for love gave me a new outlook and a new life. Love opened my dungeon and my prison. Love gave me health, more balanced emotions, a clear and broader vision. Love took me out of the underworld and has given me hundreds of earnest, loyal, and helpful friends. Love has given me an understanding wife whose intuition I can rely upon when I am tempted to bang through some red light. Love has made God available to me, and has given me a faith that works on earth as well as in Heaven. Love has banished the fear of death, confinement, and sin from my existence, and has made a future existence sure and lovely. Because God through one man loved me, I am trying to love all men. And because one man loved me, he helped me and taught me, and because of this he gave me the key to the Christian Scriptures and to the Kingdom of Heaven, to be used in proportion to my strength. By loving me he made Christ intimate and real, radiant and colourful, and life a joyous opportunity and an exciting journey. To him I pay this merited tribute: A wise counsellor, a kindly, Christ-like man who was at once my friend.

This I can say: Though many prison chaplains failed to give me the key to victory over crime, they did contribute greatly to the final outcome. For they sowed countless seeds in the barren soil of my heart. Some of these reached fallow ground and bided their season. I can recall these seeds now.

Despite the evidence I had piled up on behalf of love's transforming power, there came a day when I was on the very brink of denying the proof I possessed and the thing I inwardly knew. One of my old prison friends accosted me and began to revile me for turning tail. It was only with a supreme effort that I pressed back the old impulse to violence. He told me I was a coward. I knew I had never had more genuine courage in my life. Then he tossed a challenge at me. If I had so much courage I would go up to the chapel on our next forum day, get up on the platform, expose myself openly, and tell all my old pals the beautiful story of my changed heart. They would just love a good, old-fashioned testimonial meeting. It would be wonderful to watch me stand up for Jesus. The fellow's sarcasm was blistering. In it my life was seared and scorched and scourged.

I had never thought of this particular brand of courage. The thought of it now took the iron out of my spine and put jelly in its place. My mind bridged quickly the wide chasm of years, and once more I was facing that recitation day audience of my childhood. The whole miserable funk and fizzle was relived in a moment. A terrifying fear took hold of me. I simply didn't have the courage to do this thing. It would be another funk and another fizzle. Only that childhood ridicule would be as nothing to the belching fumes of my resentful fellow convicts.

Suddenly I had lost my moorings. The heroism of love had vanished out of my consciousness. Having departed from dependence on God, He had hidden Himself from me. I was alone with the fellow's crucifying challenge, but with an inner quaking and a display of bravery I accepted it. Having made the headlong plunge, I resolved to go through with it, no matter what the cost or outcome. Nor would I run from the test as I had done in the schoolroom.

I sent in my name and request to the forum director. Then I began to prepare my speech and to commit it to memory. It seemed that the day for my appearance would never come. I lived a million years emotionally during the short time I had to wait. I knew the speech forward and backward. I could not possibly forget it. Yet the fear that I would never ceased to haunt me.

As I sat on the platform I thought I would die. The shabbily-garbed audience was a blurred blotch as I forced my eyes over it, pretending outwardly what I belied inwardly. My imagination penetrated the blue and brought before me a huddling mass of cynical faces. The waiting suspense was martyrdom divorced from its compensating zeal. My pulses were pounding. My heart was accelerated beyond any reasonable endurance. A dense fog was in my mind.

Finally the forum director, a fellow convict, rose and began his introduction, an unnecessarily long one it seemed to me. A wave of nausea surged through me. I was trembling violently when eventually he finished and turned toward me, the cue for me to begin. How I managed to get up and out to the speaker's place, I knew not. Arriving at the appointed place I was met with a veritable bedlam of boos and catcalls, a roar of ridicule, which, like a tidal wave, broke over me again and again. Somehow I stood there waiting for it to subside. I thought I was losing consciousness. Then with an almost fiendish suddenness there came a dead hush. My mouth was dry, my tongue like a swollen chunk of celluloid. I made an effort to speak. My stiff, dry lips cracked open—but not a single word did I utter. Then came *that* laughter again, taunting, terrible, abusive, mocking. I could not take it. Once more I had failed, only my failure this time was infinitely more pronounced. I slunk from the auditorium an inglorious hero, a self-convicted coward amidst the most thunderous and murderous mockery imaginable.

By the time I was safely in my cell I was done for. I was being crowded with reasons calculated to convince me that my experience had been a delusion, and that my seeming change of heart had been a grim deception. I decided there and then to end the comedy of errors, to scuttle my resolutions, and to march straight back into the good graces of my own kind.

But I was to stand on that same platform again—not once, but many times. And I was to receive attention and respect, cheers and applause, where I had once been overwhelmed with sneers and guffaws.

And this is the protective miracle of it. Within an hour our gallery tender appeared at my cell door with a slip of paper in his hand.

"Get your things together," he said. "You're gonna move."

"Where?" I asked.

"To the other cellhouse."

"I haven't asked to move," I protested.

"I can't help that," he retorted. "I've got orders."

"Whose orders," I insisted.

"I don't know," he replied. "Just orders."

It may have been by official design that I landed in the cell with the life-termer recently mentioned, the cell into which the reader glanced in Chapter One. At any rate, the transfer protected me from the relapse I had contemplated. The lifer helped me to calm my emotions and clarify my mind. With his quieting influence I took up my prison life a wiser and a more effective aspirant of the WAY.

CHAPTER 8

MISSIONARY WORK

"SEEK THE FELLOWS YOU WANT TO HELP SILENTLY," THE LIFER told me. "But don't intrude upon those you want to help in other ways. Let this remain in God's hands. Trust in Him and He'll arrange the right time and the right place. And He'll put the right words in your mouth to fill the need. Let love precede and trust follow."

To him the missionary work was essential. But my attitude toward it in the beginning was not to be that of a pious reformer. I was not to assume the prerogative of saving others. Rather, I was to look upon others as objects upon whom I could practise love, and thereby bring about my own salvation. This attitude was certain to ward off spiritual pride, the sanctimonious air, the holier-than-thou feeling. My power and effectiveness were not to be found so much in preaching as in *being*.

I was not to ignore the historical Jesus, but release in myself more and more of the mystical Christ.

He spoke of the prison religion of the future. It would have many approaches into the moral and spiritual parts of the convict. Near the top of these would stand the missionary approach. The missionaries would be recruited from the convict body. They would be drawn from those who had *become* the message, and who were so largely integrated in themselves that love had become spontaneous dependence upon God's guidance, an automatic process.

Our discussion had started because of something I had just read concerning the trial, conviction, and execution of Jesus.

"It's all right for you to know about this outer event," he said. "But it can't do you much good to know what it means, even. What you can make of its meaning will determine your missionary effectiveness. What you know of the event can divide people by causing argument and opposition. *Before what you are in the experience and character of Christ no argument can stand, for no other proof or defence is needed. This is your light. It is this light which constrains others.*"

Then he asked me if I knew the meaning of that other incident where Jesus washed the feet of his disciples.

"You told me once that it meant humility."

"That's right, I did," he agreed. "Do you believe that's what it means?"

"Sure I do," was my prompt reply.

"And does knowing about its meaning make you humble?"

"No. I guess not."

"You see, son, you must try for the Spirit of Christ. Make no great effort to possess the theology of Christ. It is as diversified as the individuals who have it. It is Christ's attention scattered. And the theology of one man may war against the theology of another man. Leave the warfare to the theologians. It is not your field."

I was grateful for this last remark. It has saved me from many a heartbreaking disappointment.

"Try steadily to release in your experience the power which theology conceals, or embodies," he continued. "Remember it isn't your knowledge that transforms your character. You're quickened and renewed by the Spirit embodied in knowledge. Knowledge as such polishes your intellect. The Spirit quickens your soul. When the soul is quickened first, correct knowledge must follow."

He was lying sprawled on his lower bunk talking up to me.

"You just read there about Jesus being scourged. What does that mean?" he asked.

I didn't know.

"What good would it do you if you did know?" he remarked. "It might make you feel uppish. You might even impress people with your wonderful knowledge. Some might even think you were an amazing scholar of things deep and mysterious. But it'll be better when you fully experience what the scourging means. That'll come by and by. Don't worry. It'll be good for you, too. That experience will purge your character, just like a dose of Doc's salts will purge your body. Do you know what the crown of thorns meant in the passage you read?"

"No."

"Wouldn't help you much if you did," he commented.

"Might puff you up like a toad. Might even make you write a book no one could read. But when you experience the meaning of the crown of thorns, you'll release the Spirit of Christ in you. This'll make you joyous and strong. A missionary without a plan," he added significantly.

I had a feeling that he was dealing with important matters, so insistent was he upon the point of *experience as against acquired knowledge.*

"Knowing about any of these steps in the Christian Mysteries can't do you a lot of good," he repeated. "Try to realize that your real power is in the meaning as experience. You'll earn this grace as you go along."

"How?"

"Oh, by taking daily dominion. By translating knowledge into experience and experience into knowledge. And both into right action. Not by cramming so much as by emptying. If we get knowledge first, and then we're willing to give it up, we'll get wisdom instead. See! Just that simple! The best missionary is a wise man."

I heard him chuckle and his paper rattled as he picked it up. That rattling paper was the period he put on our momentary discussion. The lifer not only knew when and where to start, but he as certainly knew when and where to stop. He taught me both by precept and example.

"Have you made it change your character?"

This was the old lifer's eternal and often annoying question.

Forever and a day it was to be the test of any religious claims I might be prone to make in the future. And it would determine my prison missionary power for the production of lasting results.

In this country today there is a man who has done a little evangelistic work among underworld people, and who is a genuinely transformed and reborn man if there ever was one. He is God-sustained, God-energized, and God-guided. He preaches what he has become. Little more. Little less. He is the message he conveys. Mostly his work is inconspicuous and personal. Because of what he is, rather than because of what he knows, he has been able to redirect the lives of hundreds whom he had once resembled.

This is exactly how he got that way: he was a temporary patient in the prison hospital. The whole of his adult life had been spent in the American underworld. At that time he was serving his third prison term. He remarked to me one night that he was getting sick and tired of being society's prisoner. The remark indicated a weakened barrier, an iron door pushed partly open, a redemptive moment in his consciousness. It was my chance to give the door an added push. But I knew the moment was delicate, that I must not meet it with heady speculations and pretty generalities. He was admittedly weary of being society's prisoner, so in that moment the right thing was given me to say:

"I cut that foolishness out a year ago," I told him. "Since then I've been trying to become a prisoner of Christ. There's a big difference, buddy. If you're a prisoner of Christ it doesn't make any difference where your body is on earth. In a jail or out. In a shack or a palace. In sickness or in health. As a prisoner of Christ you're free regardless of circumstances or conditions."

And those few naked words, dropped into a receptive moment of consciousness, laid down the foundation upon which this man's life was soon destined to be completely rebuilt. In a short while he had far outshone the man who uttered the words. His redemption became my joy and my chance, another step forward in the direction of my goal, liberation through Christ.

For a number of years another man had borne the useless thorn in his flesh. Much time in prison had given him a wide and varied assortment of reading. Especially had he studied many of the frontal brain philosophies, which were aimed at the second crucifixion with art, dignity, and finesse, and at the second burial with circumlocution and inspired stupidity. To the underworld this fellow was known as "Satan," a nickname which fitted him easily, and for which he had a keen and undisguised relish. His desire to justify the name and all it stood for was obvious. His black mantle also fell in a solitary moment on a sick bed.

He had asked me to get him a Bible, saying that he wanted to hunt up a few more obvious contradictions in it. Speaking of this later he made the cryptic remark that those who press the void in order to make a case against Christ, never close the case until he does it for them.

"Search the Word that became flesh long enough," he said on another occasion, "for contradictions and denials, and you're apt to get hooked in the dragnet of hidden truth. After that you'll go fishing for men."

I brought him the Bible, which I had opened at a passage well known for its controversial content. I thought this would please Satan, since it had stopped the evolution of so many Bible scholars who had paused there to argue so loudly they could no longer hear the Master's voice calling, "What business is that of yours, follow thou me." The passage was 1 Peters 3:19. Pointing to it, I said, "Here's an interesting idea."

He took the Book, read the passage, and looked up. Then he returned to the scripture and reread it: "By which also he went and preached to the spirits in prison."

"What's so interesting about that?" he asked.

"A lot of things," I replied. "If it's traditionally true—and many including myself have reason to believe that it is—then it shows Christ not just as a friend to the prisoners but a very special friend."

"What's your reason for believing it to be true?" he asked.

"I was in prison and he came to me," I quoted. "I know others in prison he's come to."

"How?" Satan asked.

"In His Spirit," I told him.

"I don't see it," he said in a prompting tone.

I explained that the time Christ preached to the prisoners as here recorded was a very special time in his life and ministry. It was during those mysterious three days between the Crucifixion and the Resurrection. So he must have been free of his mortal body. The place where the prisoners were confined was called Hell or Hades. This place stood for the lowest hells of the earth plane. It was far below the level on which ordinary society lived. "Are you interested?" I asked.

"Go right ahead," he replied. "I'm all ears."

"O.K., then. You asked for it."

I told him that in order for Christ to visit the hell-bound spirits he had to descend into the most miserable conditions imaginable. He did this as a voluntary sacrifice, and it proved his unlimited love for the imprisoned population. These vile prison hellholes still existed.

I paused here a moment. Then: "And Christ, insulted, spurned, spat on, abused, and repulsed by the very ones he came to help, is still descending into the filthy hells as a friend and redeemer of all the miserable, ignorant, half-witted saps like us who burn and roast in them."

Now Satan was not without rationality and intelligence, though he had failed to live according to intelligent self-interest. He pondered this scripture, as he lay there alone on his sick bed. He considered all the "ifs" and "ands" and the "pros" and the "cons" and the "yeas" and the "nays" of theology. It was true that he could make this passage look like a dime's worth of dog meat if he had a mind to. But his meditation drew him below the crusty surface of controversy and argument. None of that type of thinking had any transforming power in it, which he well knew. So he took it just as it was written, and reached the inner conviction that if Christ loved the prisoners well enough to join them in their hellholes they in turn ought to love him. There and then he made a mental decision to become a prisoner of Christ instead of Satan. He ceased to be a dispenser of the antichrist philosophy. His nickname, a symbol of false pride and disgrace, in due time faded away for lack of attention, and he lived to win recognition and respect for the name conferred upon him by the mystery of birth.

I know this man well. He is today a respectable and respected member of society. And I can truthfully say that out of this one text he built up a case for the transforming Christ that was so persuasive, brilliant, and logical that it turned scores of bad actors around in their tracks. And for anyone to reduce this sublime text to the level of fruitless haggling in his presence was to court disaster.

For the confirmed and hardened criminal, Christ and all that he implies holds out a sure hope and offers a certain way out of the swamplands of defeat and useless misery. However, Satan's was a mild case of the antisocial character and anti-spiritual personality when compared with the following one:

This convict—we knew him as Parson Jack—had had the advantage of a Christian home, theological education, and Christian training. He became what might be called a religious intellectual. He later referred to this period of his life as a hodgepodge of nothing *plus*. He had been so busy studying religion that he had had no time left for its practice. He had been so eager to prepare himself academically to serve others, that he had failed to see that his first service was to himself. He made the mistake of assuming others as an end for his service, instead of as a means for furthering his own improvement. Others were to be reformed by him. He was not to be reformed by them. The faults of others distressed him. His own disturbed him not.

The upshot of his career was—and he was a mature man when it happened—that he came to a sudden and painful recognition that something was wrong. He didn't know that it was his attitude. He only knew that with all his polish and intellectual equipment he had not been able to win a single soul for Christ. He could attract the admiration of others, but he could not melt and move their hearts. His appeal was wholly mental, and though as such it was successful, from the standpoint of religious experience he knew it was pathetic, futile, tragic. People unwittingly crucified him with praise. They said that he could make them think. But deep down within him he knew that religious experience was far more than thinking. It was thinking plus feeling plus knowing. To *think* the presence of Christ was without transforming power; but to *feel* the presence of Christ was to know him and be known by him.

Finally there came to this man a bitter sense of frustration. He did not have the correct attitude, nor did he possess that which he urged upon others. He was minus in both departments. His inner conflict was set into motion, and here again he failed utterly to recognize the meaning and value of spiritual conflict. So instead of allowing the conflict to push him on toward the inevitable crisis, Parson Jack went into a tailspin of protest and revolt. Had he not done this, at the point of crisis, he would have been driven to despair and an unqualified mental surrender to God. By revolt he sought to escape the very thing that harboured his victory.

He turned away into strange fields. He began to pursue odd and unusual religious substitutes, queer philosophical piracies out of the East, "manufactured for Western world export," and other current systems calculated further to exalt the Cain of pride and to suppress the Abel of meekness and compassion, systems determined to keep the musty banner of self-importance hoisted above the simple transparency of the pure life.

These escape paths brought him eventually to the wayward son of a Lutheran minister. At the feet of Nietzsche, whose philosophy has since captured three fourths of the Christian world, Parson Jack laid down his soul—Nietzsche, who had become a Swiss professor and popularizer of the bizarre *superman,* who converted pride into a crown rather than a cross. With this newly discovered preceptor Parson Jack began to see eye to eye. Sin became beautiful, and everything that bowed in affirmation to the unregenerate instincts and animal appetites became admirable.

As a result Parson Jack grew even more brilliant, egotistical, amazingly earnest and amazingly more superficial. The great Antichrist's *Beyond Good and Evil* became not the preliminary mutterings of a future madman, but the dream of a "saviour" who offered heaven on earth in return for saying "yes" to human desire and "no" to everything else. And Nietzsche's book, *Thus Spake Zarathustra,* became an unconditional substitute for the Christian Bible. The leadership of the Antichrist himself became Parson Jack's substitute for the wise, perfected, pure, and gentle Nazarene.

It was an extraordinary substitution. Here was idol worship gone wild, the reasons for which would befuddle the best psychologist who made a speciality of the odd in religious practice. And what an idol! A confused man of "the higher learning" preaching the tawdry, old doctrine of might over right, of the domineering intellect over the compassionate heart, giving the recently developed forebrain regnancy, and the old, old heart the office of court fool, but with a warped genius capable of influencing millions of sane, normal people with a mouldy and disgraceful plagiarism.

Here was an idol who thought of sin as freedom, of violence as character; an idol gone raving mad on the empty husks of his own devitalized precepts; an idol with an unspeakable taint in his blood; one who, as Papini pointed out, voiced in his last letter the most appalling assumption ever conceived in a sick and twisted mind, by calling himself, "The Crucified One."

Nietzsche gave Parson Jack a monumental disrespect for the rights of others, and Jack trailed his idol straight to the hard steel gates of prison. In fact, he became a constant repeater of offence. And for years he preached the fuzzy gospel of negation while he checked off his days behind stone walls. The humour in his preachments eluded him entirely. He was wholly sincere in his astonishing self-deception. Misused words had acted upon him as a narcotic drug. Parson Jack took his *superman* seriously, in spite of the guarded smiles of his fellows, who were less susceptible to the grotesque and ridiculous. But he was destined, like the Prodigal, to come to himself. His Christian background and religious training were not to be denied forever.

We met, the Parson and I, on the playground one Saturday afternoon. Indirectly, and with a certain respect for my old reputation, Parson Jack accused me of a number of right-about-faces, which I was happy to admit. He knew, of course, that I was now advocating the "love theory" among the "more impressionable convicts," so he had waited his chance to corner me where he could explode this fallacy once and for all time.

"There's a rumour going around," he said, "that God is love." But he got no further. I was ready to move on. I left him with my answer, however:

"He must be love, Jack. Had he been anything else He'd have pulled our lying and conceited tongues out years ago. Only love could say we're fit to live. Justice couldn't say it." With this I walked away after waiting for a moment for his answer, which didn't come.

For suddenly Parson Jack found himself in a stuttering, ineffectual position. The bullet had hit the target. He resented my remark bitterly—but it stuck. He could have knifed me there and then, had he been that cowardly. Instead he was forced to swallow the remark and to face the truth in it. Nor was this facing up to the truth to let him go. When the inner war had subsided and he had regained a measure of calm judgment, he performed the first courageous act he had done in many years. He came to me with a testimony on his lips, telling me I was right. And later he performed an infinitely more courageous act: he stood on the chapel platform and shared his experience with a sardonic and cynical audience of fellow convicts. He told us of his return to prayer after a lapse of years. It was a curious prayer, which I remember in effect, though not, of course, in his exact words.

"Father, I'm confused, terribly confused," he said, as he knelt beside his bunk. "I don't know what it's all about. Right now I've got a big war inside of me, but I don't feel an ounce of repentance. If that's necessary you can make me feel it, if you want to. I don't even know what it is, but I'm praying just the same. In your Word you've challenged me to prove you. I don't know how. This is the best I can do. I doubt if I'm even sincere. You know what's in my heart—I don't. If I'm not sincere I can't help it. There's no one can make me sincere but you. I know that much all right. If you want me to be sincere you can change me mighty quick. And you're the only one who can."

As Parson Jack testified along this line, absolutely honest, sincere, truthful with himself, a profound hush settled over the audience of faces that previously had been very smug in their scepticism. There was an involuntary leaning forward.

"I'm a weakling, Father," Jack continued. "I'm a sinner, but I don't know what sin is or what it's for. I don't know why I'm a sinner and others are not. I've a mighty strong hunch that I'm not altogether to blame. I know this, that you made me, and I know you can remake me if you're not satisfied. As far as I know you're just as much to blame as I am for my failure. I know you could have prevented all this crazy nonsense I've plowed through, but you didn't see fit to turn a hand. And you can do away with it right now if you don't like it. I hope you don't. It isn't a matter of faith—I know that. If you want to change me you can do it. I'm making no promises, no bargains—I'm too weak. I don't know how to do it anyway. I'm just saying you could have prevented this mess; that you can change it all now, if you want to. I can't do it alone—I don't know how. I haven't got what it takes. You have. If you want me to do your will you'll give me the secret and the strength, and I aim to keep right on talking to you till you hear me, even if it takes the rest of my life."

None of us had ever heard a prayer in this vein. Parson Jack insisted that it was not irreverent. As he stated it, he was just talking turkey to God, minus a funereal air and long face.

He didn't tell us how God answered his prayer, but it was an unmistakable fact, plain to everybody, that this man had undergone a revolutionary change. He was a wholly different person with a wholly different preachment on his lips. And I personally know that his testimony that day had its effect on several confirmed criminals who later left prison to return no more.

The prison missionary has this in his favour: it is the common belief of convicts that institutional methods cannot correct a criminal character, once that character has been formed and set. In my own attempts at missionary work, therefore, I wasted no time trying to clarify penological theories, but went straight to the redemptive power of Christ. I was successful to the degree I attained that power within myself, and in the measure of my personal experience to speak with authority. I cannot explain this, except to say that when I was in the power of God my efforts were effective; otherwise they always failed.

There are many obstacles which stand between the convict and Christ. Of these the most common and most difficult is that of a misconception, due to the confusion that exists between the practice of Christianity and the demands of its Founder. In his cell the criminal feels that because an intolerant Christianity has ostracized him, and has branded him with a stigma that he is likewise unacceptable to Christ himself. The removal of this one obstacle would mark the difference between an effective prison religion and that which is now and has been in existence. The elimination of this barrier has brought many a tough customer into the Shepherd's eternal fold.

In my own practice of Christ through the medium of service the lifer told me to keep this point always in mind—I still do. *My argument was and is that Christ must be a special friend to the criminal, the dispossessed, the outcasts of earth, because these, in many respects, seem to have greater need for his transforming touch, and that Christian society has nothing whatever to do with it, that Christian society, in fact, by rejecting the criminal and his Christian needs, is actually rejecting the Christ it proclaims to adore and embrace.*

As an example of this personal procedure I recall the case of a first offender. Paul was a sensitive and likeable fellow who possessed talent and a deep, thoughtful nature. He had great possibilities for good which, misdirected, were equally as great for the execution of evil. The experience, which ended in his trial, conviction, and imprisonment, had embittered him until the mere mention of religion was sufficient to arouse his hatred. He believed that he had been divorced from Christ because, as he claimed, he had been convicted by a Christian jury, testified against by a group of Christian witnesses, lied about by a Christian prosecutor, sentenced and reviled by a Christian judge, and finally imprisoned under a Christian jailer.

It was necessary to explain to him, not in sweet sentimental Christian accents, but in iron-blooded Christian logic, that he had built the wall between himself and God, and that no one else had anything whatever to do with it. He had to be shown that a Christian society did not necessarily mean a Christ-like society; that Christian claims did not necessarily constitute a Christ-like life; that no Christian pretences could in any way alter the central fact of Christ and of his redeeming grace and love.

However, this line of reasoning had to be backed up with authority. It was pointed out to him that Peter was the first called. And then he was asked, "Who was the first to have the honour and glory of accompanying the Master into Paradise?"

"Why, it was a thief," Paul exclaimed, suddenly aware of a very old fact.

"It was a criminal," I repeated, "an outcast who bore the social stigma of those days; a man rejected by society was accepted by the only perfect member society has ever known."

"I'd never thought of that," Paul replied seriously. And with this statement his attitude towards Christ was changed.

To another like him I pointed out the cosmic importance of the Resurrection scene. Then I asked him: "To whom did the Risen Lord first identify himself after his conquest of death?"

"To Mary Magdalene," he replied correctly.

"To Mary, the outcast," I added. "Never forget it." And he didn't.

I found out in my prison missionary work that if I met the requirements of love and trust the correct thing would invariably be given to me to say. Always this fitted the individual case, and filled the individual need. Sometimes the good results were quick and startling. Other times the spoken words were like seeds planted in soil that had suddenly become fertile. Always I felt an upward surge in myself when the subject of my effort caught the vision and was stirred with a strange new impulse rising out of his quickened soul.

This manner of practising the Presence of God was, as the lifer assured me, highly profitable from every angle. When I would relate the results in the case of some old offender, he would smile and say, "That one alone makes amends for all your offences against society."

This was the sort of thing he called, "making true retribution."

CHAPTER 9

MY RETURN TO HEALTH

WHEN I WENT INTO THE OLD LIFER'S CELL THE RAVAGES OF my life of crime and dissipation were upon me and within me. The dungeon experience had discovered my soul; but only time and effort could recover the health I had so lavishly and foolishly squandered.

My kidneys and liver were in bad shape. A dangerously depleted pancreas had thrown across my life the shadow of diabetes. My lungs were a constant temptation to the White Scourge germs. My heart was still labouring with a heavy blood stream and extremities which were consistently cold. Both my stomach and bladder were tender and hot. There were guarded whispers going about that I was done for, that I knew this fact, and it was hinted that herein was the real reason for my *turning religious.*

To say that I was not alarmed about the state of my health would be a falsehood. I was alarmed. And now, as never before, I had a passionate desire to live. It seemed that for the first time in my whole life I had something for which to live. There was a future. Amends were to be made. A worthwhile life was to be attained. I was old and broken in body, but I was still young in years, in mind, and in spirit. I wanted eagerly to regain my bodily health and vigour and to devote this recovered health to an active life programme of constructive living.

The old lifer mentioned that I did not seem well. I, in turn, mentioned my desire to be well.

"There are healing agents in the world," he said, "both visible and invisible. The whole healing art is a ministry, one of the noblest and

109

greatest of them all. Because of this ministry every man has a chance to live right up to his last minute at work."

His words and his spirit inspired instant hope in me.

"All healers," he went on, "no matter in what branch of the art they minister, are under the will of God. To the medical scientist He gives the skill and the medicine; to the psychologist the power of suggestion; to the disciple of Christ the gift of love and faith and the grace of prayer. They are all at your disposal. Respect them all for what they are, ministers. And remember always the Healer behind the healers. He who has said, 'I am the Lord that healeth thee.' This will give you the right attitude towards *the* Healer and His ministers."

Each morning found me in the sick-call line. Where I had once looked upon the prison doctor with contempt, as a "croaker" and dispenser of liquid murder, I now saw in him a minister who, unconsciously perhaps, was practising the will of God through the sick and pain-shot bodies of crime-ridden men. My admiration for the doctor rose. Before the healing power which he embodied, I stood in reverent awe. His response to my attitude was prompt. He put his knowledge, his humanity, and all his healing equipment at my disposal, just as the lifer had said he would do when my attitude was right.

Our resident psychiatrist gave over each Thursday to those who had voluntarily requested interviews. The man I had loathed as a racketeer, I now sought as a minister of God. I looked forward to my weekly visit, and he told me frankly that he shared my sentiment. Between us there was no longer a professional wall. Freely I supplied him with knowledge concerning the subtler phases of the criminal mind, which he could not otherwise obtain. In return he gave me all that he knew about the salutary use of autosuggestion. And he freely shared the results of his academic and laboratory experience.

The prison chaplain, whom I had once despised, became my friend. When my feeling towards him changed, his feeling towards me changed. Friendship, I was to discover, became a great mental clarifier. As one who hated him, I had seen in the chaplain a religious hypocrite who was willing to sell his soul for a soft job and political favour. I had heard in his sermons nothing but a lot of stale generalities and ecclesiastical balderdash. As his friend I saw him as a man struggling with great personal and family problems; a man of quick sympathies for the suffering of others; a chaplain, though handicapped by all sorts of red tape and opposition, eager to be of service to his God through men. With a friendly ear I found in his sermons amazing expositions of Truth and Revelation, and I wondered if he had been reborn, for it was not the chaplain making these inspired utterances, but God making them through him.

"No, he's about the same," the lifer said, when I inquired of him concerning the matter. "Your change has made the difference. Hate, though having ears, cannot hear. Through the ears of love all things become illumined, and that which the world calls trite glows with a huge significance."

With his elbows leaning against the bars of our cell, the chaplain stood chatting one noontime. No one had ever heard him express himself on the issue of spiritual healing, as that issue affected his own church and creed. I was sitting on a stool. The lifer was lying on his bunk. Suddenly I felt moved to ask: "Will you pray for my health, chaplain?"

The lifer's hand came out and covered one of mine. The pressure told me plainer than words that he was pleased with my frank and honest request.

"Chaplain," he said, "if you'll just seek first the kingdom for him, if your prayer is for the health of his soul, then maybe the health of his body will be added."

Swift tears came to the chaplain's eyes. His voice was husky when he spoke. "I'll gladly pray for both," he said. "You've made me mighty happy. This sacred trust alone banishes every disappointment the office of chaplain has given me."

Thus was I swung into the orbit of health and healing through the three grand departments of the same divine art. The lifer did his share.

One evening he came into the cell with a group of character pictures. Apparently he had been searching through discarded movie and confession magazines until he had accumulated the pictures he wanted.

He handed one of them to me and told me to observe it closely. It was the picture of what had once been a man. Now it was a horrible and horrifying creature of lust and greed. He was bending over a table in a dingy room. His eyes were small and beady, his face sharp and avaricious, as he gazed fixedly at the pile of coins he was counting.

"I'd say this guy would turn a mule's stomach," was my response.

"It's an accurate picture," the lifer replied, "of the miser. He's loved money in the wrong way. We become like the thing we love."

The next picture was that of a woman. Every feature on her coarse, ugly face revealed the chronic gossiper, the evil and malicious peddler of tales. I passed it back to him quickly with no comment.

"The typical gossip," he observed. "No one could mistake her. She's become like the thing she loves." He handed me another.

It was another woman. Her skinny, bent form, and bloodless body told the story of constant illness. She was talking enthusiastically to three bored but polite neighbours—talking about her poor health. Self-pity, and self-sustained invalidism were written all over her, in her manner, in the hangdog cast of her eyes, the droop of her unkempt head.

"She's become like the thing she loves," said the lifer humorously. *"The hardest thing in the world is to maintain ill health. You've got to live constantly in the sick thought if you're to defeat Nature's re-creative power."*

Next he gave me a cut. I knew, of course, where he had obtained this. It had come from the prison office of identification. It was a cut of myself, taken three days after I had entered upon my present sentence.

"Do I look that bad?" I asked.

112

"You did," he replied. "But not now. An inner change brings a corresponding outer reflection. When that picture was taken you were a typical criminal, narrow, intolerant, hateful, and selfish. A detective could smell you a mile away. Your trade was stamped in every tissue of your body. Any child would have mistrusted you. You were a hardened criminal. You had become the image of the thing you loved."

The next picture was that of a very old lady. She was sitting in a wheelchair. Her invalidism, though obvious, did not attract attention. Two children were at her knees, and she was reading *Pilgrim's Progress* to them. Through her aged body was reflected a nameless health and youthfulness. Her face glowed with an unspeakable vitality and peace. Her eyes twinkled. No sick thought found lodgement in her mind. She gave one a sense of purity and saintliness, of supreme conquest and victory over the world and her own aged condition. To take her hand would be to declare, "I felt eternal life in that touch."

"She's become like the thing she loves," the lifer said.

Then there was a picture of a man by the name of Edison. He had been snapped at his work. The picture could have been studied for a lifetime without producing a negative observation or reaction.

"He's become like the thing he loves," he remarked. "What do the pictures tell you?" he asked. Then he gave the answer.

"If you love health enough, you have a mighty good chance of becoming healthy in all your parts; physical, emotional, mental, and spiritual. We'll try to keep you so much in the health thought that the sick thought will in time be crowded out."

Toward this end a three-point programme was evolved for me, which dealt with the practice of relaxation, concentration, and meditation.

With the aid of these and with the aid of the prison doctor, the resident psychiatrist, the chaplain, and the lifer, the seemingly impossible was achieved in my body, and I became a well and life-glad man.

CHAPTER 10

THE ACTION OF INACTION

Love alone introduces God to me. Love is my sanctuary—in factory, field, city street; in bedroom, office, kitchen, sick room. I have my sanctuary everywhere I go in the Universe. Where love is, there God is. —Toyohiko Kagawa

"TO KNOW HOW NOT TO ACT IS TO KNOW HOW AND WHEN to act." This was one of the lifer's favourite aphorisms. It implied self-dominion, not by self-mastery, but by self-surrender, not by will force, but by will power; the former being man's prerogative—the latter, God's. The one resisted everything and took dominion over nothing: the other resisted nothing and took dominion over everything. The first rebelled against opposition: the second embraced it. That man was to resist evil courted no argument, but the question hinged on how it was to be accomplished.

"Resist evil and it will flee from you," the lifer quoted. "This implies both force and fear. For the moment you are protected from the evil, but the condition which attracts it has not been corrected. Society resists the evil of crime in this manner, puts the evildoer away for a season, and then breathes easily. But one day the prison doors will open and the evildoer will again come forth to stalk his prey. The condition has not been corrected. Nothing has been overcome. Finally evil must be overcome with good. The conquest of sin waits upon man's capacity to function in spiritual love."

In this same connection Amiel wrote in his Journal: "Do not hope to excite love except by love. Be what you wish others to become. Let yourself and not your words preach for you."

But how to become what you wish others to become, how to possess the love that will excite love in others, how to obtain the feeling to approach feeling! This brings us to practice and to the very perfume and soul of the lifer's convictions. If science is insufficient to produce redemption, then how may it become sufficient? This involves practice, which precedes example; practice with a strong purpose, for repetition without purpose produces little or no improvement. If healing and salvation depend upon love, and love is absent, shall we do nothing at all about it? Or can we by purposeful practice evoke love within ourselves, and thus excite love in others?

The lifer's answer was "yes" to this. The example I have recounted concerning Guard Peters and me bears out his conviction; this book and my life testify to the soundness and effectiveness of the old lifer's methods and practices.

Of the numerous ways he presented to approach love while still being divorced from love, that of active inaction was among my most pleasurable practices. It involved an ability to translate thinking into feeling. These were quiet times. We practised together three times daily, morning, noon, and night.

Since the nature of love was warmth, this quiet time practice had to do with producing the feeling of warmth by a direct exercise of the will. When the feeling of warmth was thus produced in the body it acted as a healing and purifying agent, both in the physical and emotional parts. In other words, it was a superphysical method of self-treatment.

Medical science is now employing a similar but very limited technique in the treatment of certain organic diseases by the application of artificial heat which produces artificial fever. This, of course, is not likely to effect any change in the patient's physical habits, or his mental and emotional states. Whereas the other method, if persisted in with purpose and enthusiasm over a period of time, certainly will effect such changes, it will also, in time, evoke a genuine feeling of love, which in turn will excite love, in God as well as in man.

My experience has been that many of the current metaphysical methods advanced for self-treatment do defeat their purpose in that they are often too potent and result in stirring up lusts and passions and other emotional dregs without dissolving them. Rarely, however, have I experienced this effect during any of my quiet times where the purpose has been to produce the feeling of warmth.

Science, philosophy, art, and religion all are methods of practice which aim at some sort of healing in the individual or in the collective relationships. Science, philosophy, and art are motivated by love and thus produced healing, but only to the depth of the *ego*. Religion, in its true sense, is love, and a love which rises not out of the *ego* but out of the soul. Hence in religion as love there is redemption, salvation, the supreme healing.

The scientific attitude is nothing more nor less than an insatiable love for the recovery of truth, which, when found, heals the consciousness of error. But this love is still relative to religion, and consequently is incapable of recovering more than relative truth. In its purely social aspect there is an expansion of love with a corresponding looseness of scientific method.

Philosophy is nothing more nor less than an insatiable love for making truth more generally available. It is, when it does not break over into the orbit of religion, the handmaiden of science. It is perhaps correct to say that not more than five per cent of the world's articulate population can read and understand a scientific formula. The philosopher can, through expository elaboration, increase this percentage to ten, and in some instances to even fifteen or twenty per cent.

Art has behind it the same insatiable love for truth, and it is the true mission of art to re-embody the relative truth discovered by science and explained by philosophy into forms and actions which, when presented, can be enjoyed and understood by all civilized people, and in some cases by those who are not civilized. Art is, therefore, the parable-maker for science and philosophy.

Jesus was able to do for the spiritual world what science, philosophy, and art are able to do for the relative world: he could uncover ultimate truth and state it to a few advanced disciples, expound it to another five or ten per cent of the people, and finally re-embody it into parables, thus making it available to all the people.

The lifer's vision saw growth in the human family as an endless series of healings. To advance to a new part, one was automatically healed in the old part. *Where others saw sin as a tragedy, he saw it as an opportunity. Because of sin there was the need of healing, and because there was a need of healing there was a need of the healing agent, and in the final analysis this healing agent was love.*

To him sin was simply a word which gathered up all negative conditions into one big body and which finally must be healed. In the meantime sin compelled man to bring about its own elimination; it furnished opposition necessary for growth, and when seen as opportunity, it invoked love and released wisdom. Because of sin there was a need of wisdom and love, and so long as wisdom and love were needed they were available. Being available salvation was possible; the soul's ultimate liberation was certain.

Our quiet times, therefore, were made possible because of sin. There was something to overcome, something to heal. In these periods we were simply meeting opposition with non-resistance. It was one of many methods or practices he taught me for taking dominion over sin. The feeling of warmth evoked, according to the lifer, had the power to melt out or dissolve much that was active and inactive in the great sin body to which we were subjected and by which our souls were opposed.

There were two groups of sins, especially, which focused the attention of the old lifer: these were the secret sins of the imagination, and the crystallized sins, or the so-called respectable sins that were commonly accepted as harmless and were taken generally for granted.

In the quiet time God's penetrating searchlight was apt to single out these particular groups, expose them to our conscience, and shame us with the dominion we had given them in our lives.

James I. Vance, writing of the sins of the imagination in his *The Rise of a Soul*, gave this description: "The sins of the imagination hide under cover. They are secret infamies. They inhabit the underworld, hugging the darkness and cloaking with concealment; but they are all the more dangerous to the soul, because so subtle."

These are the sins which people feed on in secret, while outwardly they are wrapped in the mantle of a sanctimonious air. Jesus condemned such sinning as hypocritical. It was white with the bleached bones of self-deception and false pride. It was the act of cowardice, for it offered vicarious sense gratification to persons who feared the judgment of other sinners more than they feared the merciful judgment of God. In my long years in crime I had come to question the motives of social workers who, by this means, were able to fraternize with criminals without courting the critical judgment of men. There are secret criminals who, outwardly, are of good character. That God knows them for what they are inwardly is not important. It is well, so long as man does not find them out. "Dangerous to the soul, because so subtle."

It was in these quiet times with the lifer that my sins of the imagination were exposed. But I can honestly and gratefully say that the method which exposed them likewise did much toward their healing. So far as I am concerned the sins of the imagination are the most dangerous to the soul, the subtlest, and will be the last to vanish from man's life.

The key passage of scripture he used was found in Matthew 5:39. He prefaced every quiet period with a vocal declaration of it: "But I say unto you, that ye resist not evil."

In other words, put up no resistance, but let God's searchlight probe relentlessly into your heart, and bring every corner of secret sin out into the full glare of exposure, to be dissolved in the warmth you have evoked, to be sublimated, transformed in the glow of your finer feelings.

The so-called respectable sins had chiefly to do with the cheap and tawdry attitudes man embraced and the crude negative reactions he permitted.

"Don't lay claim to salvation," he told me, "so long as gossip still appeals to you, so long as you're more disturbed by the faults of others than by your own, so long as you can still excuse your own weakness, and shift your own blame to another."

The old lifer taught me the secret of being inwardly active in an outward calm. For this I owe him much. In the warm glow of this place of peace many oppositions have vanished, many, many healings have come to me.

CHAPTER 11

CHRIST'S WAY AS MAN'S CHANCE

TO THE LIFER, GOD WAS EVER A CHALLENGE TO MAN, AND THE way of Christ was ever the answer to that challenge. He seemed always to hear God calling, "Prove Me," and Jesus declaring, "In earth as in heaven."

It was not that he insisted on a practical application of the gospels at all points; but that he emphasized the necessity of making the teachings of Jesus work in the world first. He felt that the Christian mysteries would unfold to the man who had taken a measure of self-dominion by the conscious application of love. He often told me that no man was worthy of being a custodian of the mysteries of God who had proven himself incapable of making a practical success on the basis of the Golden Rule.

He believed, also, that a man could best attain to an effective social gospel by the avenue of a personal gospel; that is, in his opinion, if a person unfolded his latent spiritual capacities first, without any particular reference to their social implications, he would then assume his social ministry naturally and with more power.

Here he stood upon the authority of the Master's example rather than upon his precept. He prepared his disciples before he crowned them with power. Endued with power, they could not only take up the social gospel and save souls but they were organically fine enough and strong enough to be trusted with the Christian Mysteries. It was given to them to understand the mysteries of God. It was likewise given to them to teach these mysteries to others by the use of apt parables and concrete illustrations.

Hence the old lifer's teaching method in connection with me was first of all personal and practical. *"Genuine Revelation will come,"* he once said, *"when you're able to contain it without show or without pride."* In the beginning, therefore, the social gospel was to be considered merely as my chance to help myself. That is, I was not to consider others as objects to be helped by me, but as opportunities for me to practise the Master's teachings in an effort to improve myself. If, in this process, those were aided upon whom I practised, I was to count this as a special grace and a special joy.

The lifer often uncovered opportunities for practice, which he would pass on to me. For instance, there was a coloured boy who was a porter in our shop. He had gotten himself into grave difficulties with a white girl outside, not necessarily by deceiving her, but rather by allowing her to deceive herself.

This girl had yielded to the appeal of a social worker and had accepted a small list of prisoners with whom she promised to correspond. Her intentions were good. She had in mind the possibility of helping forgotten men. But she hadn't considered the state of her own emotions nor those of the average prisoner.

On her list of names was Jug, our porter. Now Jug, during his months in prison, had become an accomplished composer of letters. As time went on and the correspondence continued, the girl's list of names decreased until but one name remained. Jug had cleared the field of all competition. At this point the romantic note entered into the correspondence with unveiled boldness. The white girl became emotionally involved, and Jug himself, thoroughly starved in his emotional life, was lured into deeper and deeper play with the ball of fire he had set into motion. From his angle the affair was a life-saver, since it gave him an outlet for his restricted feelings. What he did not anticipate, however, was the girl's decision to visit him, and thus discover that he was not the white man whom she had supposed him to be.

This was Jug's problem, and by its very nature it was a problem difficult to confide. The girl was determined to pay him a visit, and apparently there was nothing Jug could do to prevent what he thought to be a coming tragedy.

In his desperation he cornered the lifer and revealed the predicament he was in. The latter immediately saw that much more was involved than Jug suspected. The girl's reaction could not be predicted. She might take it without much disappointment, while again she might think she had been frightfully deceived by Jug and react in such a way as to cause trouble for the prison officials who granted such indiscriminate writing privileges to the convicts. This, in turn, would react against all the other prisoners, who enjoyed outside correspondence, the special privilege would be denied them and the old restrictions on letter writing would be imposed.

The lifer passed the problem on to me. "Human love," he commented with a broad grin, "can get us into hot water. But human love spiritualized puts the good Lord into action. Poor Jug's in a jam. Whatta ya suppose the old boy can do about it?"

I began to think of loopholes and detours.

"Would Christ meet the problem with compromise and further deception?" he asked.

"No," I affirmed.

"How would he meet it then?"

"Well, he'd be honest with his own soul. I don't know how he'd get around it. It looks like a tough spot for Jug and everybody else in here. I guess Jug ought to write the girl and make a clean breast of the whole thing."

"We can't tell how the girl would take it," he said. "She might write a scorching letter to the warden. You know what that would mean."

"There's nothing anyone can do that I can see," I told him. "Looks to me like one of those problems that leaves a guy stripped. It's like being mentally handcuffed."

The old lifer was smiling enigmatically now as he walked back and forth. "Why are you smiling?" I asked.

"Well," he replied, "I'm smiling because I'm happy. I'm happy because this is a perfect opportunity for me to teach you a lesson on prayer."

"On prayer?"

"Yep. That's it—on prayer. I believe," he said, "that we should never try to make a crutch out of God. He's given us faculties and powers to do certain things ourselves, and to do them righteously. But there's a limit to these. At the point where we can do no more ourselves, what should we do?"

"Pray?" I asked.

"Yes," he said. "At this point we should stop trying, and give the whole thing to God. Utterly. Uncompromisingly. Completely surrender it up to Him."

"Is this what Jug should do?" I asked.

"Maybe Jug doesn't know how to do it. Then what?"

"You can't prove it by me," I admitted.

"There is such a thing as intercessory prayer," he explained. "That's when someone prays for someone else. For instance, if we prayed for Jug and the girl and surrendered their problem to God, that would be intercessory prayer."

"Let's pray for them," I said.

"Could we do it in Christ's name?" he asked.

"Couldn't we?" I asked in turn.

"Yes," he said, "if the thing we pray for is approved by Christ. Do you think Christ would approve if we gave this problem to God, and thanked Him for its solution? You know the Master dealt with such human problems himself."

"Then he'd approve, wouldn't he, since there seems no other way to solve the thing?"

"Well, we'll take a chance on it," said he. "Come on down here. We're gonna do this thing right. We're gonna get right down on our prayer bones. But first of all, let's be sure we have no pet prejudices in the matter. Let's be sure we love both Jug and the girl in a big, fine way as we think God would love them. How do you feel about Jug?"

"Sorry for him, I guess. But I've always liked Jug. And I wouldn't want to see the girl hurt. And I wouldn't want to see all the other guys in here lose their writing privileges."

"That's okay. Just kneel down here at the bunk beside me, and I'll talk to the Father about it."

As he prayed I felt power being released as though from within me. He could not have prayed over a few minutes, yet before he had finished I experienced a quiet sense of inner assurance, which seemed to want to express itself in some such words as "It is done," or "It is finished," or "Everything is all right."

Immediately after the prayer, he shifted the subject to a topic wholly foreign to the one under discussion. He began to tell me about a daring escape that had been made years before. It was an exciting tale, and under the spell of his dramatic ability, I lost all connection with the problem of Jug and his white girl correspondent.

About two weeks later the girl came to the prison to visit Jug. He turned almost white when the keeper handed him the visitor's slip. But the lifer had told him that if she came to go on up and ask her forgiveness. He followed these instructions, and the girl not only forgave him but did it graciously, taking it all as good fun and high adventure. She, herself, suggested that they continue to correspond, rather than break off abruptly. This was carried out. The correspondence was placed on a beautiful and more impersonal level, with the result that the girl had such a pronounced influence over Jug for good that his life became very much changed. And my faith in the power of prayer took a decided lift upward!

One evening the lifer told me that to have dominion over oneself and one's world was to put the word of love to work. I was to see a concrete proof of this before bedtime. The proof gave me the stimulation that comes with a new and sudden Revelation.

We had a night keeper in our cell house by the name of Peters. Now it so happened that I did not particularly like Peters, and Guard Peters apparently had no particular liking for me. He had never spoken to me unofficially. But, in passing our cell on his rounds of duty, he often stopped to chat a moment with my cell buddy.

So after I'd had time to think over the lesson of the previous night, and to sort of digest what the lifer had said about putting love to work, I got up on my bunk and began to think of the stiff relations between Peters and me. I said to the old lifer, "Why does Peters dislike me?" He replied that I had the question in the wrong person, and that it should be, "Why do I dislike Guard Peters?"

As I sought to turn up the answer to this latter question, I found that it was most difficult and elusive. I concluded that my dislike for the keeper was due mostly to the long years of enmity and prejudice I had entertained for all emissaries of the law. I related this conclusion to him. He cocked his head at a quizzical angle, pursed and stroked his lips in a reflective manner, and said that I was probably right.

"But," he added, "people do have instant likes and dislikes. So there might be a deeper reason, just as there's a deeper reason for crime than that known to the social experts. Now between you and Peters there's a barrier. Neither of you can see it, but it's there. It's just like the barrier between the social world and the underworld, which neither the criminal nor society can see. It is intangible but it's a fact. You have been looking at the worst in Peters, and he has been letting you see the thing you have looked for."

He assured me that this observation might be wrong, however. Then he suggested that I try reversing the process and go to looking for the best in Peters, just to see what would come of it. "See if you can find the Image of God in him," he finished.

"But how?" I asked.

"By simply using your imaging faculty," he replied, "your imagination. You've got one or you wouldn't be here. Every con in the place is the victim of his misused imagination. This isn't so hard to do if you really try."

With this he fell into the parabolic method of speaking. He brought forth the common camera to illustrate his point. He said that when the eye of the camera was focused on an object, and the shutter was clicked, the image of the object would be printed on the negative film inside.

"But the image is not clear," he said, "is it?"

"No."

"Well, it's there just the same. And if you know the object focused upon you can easily see the image on the negative through the inner eye of your imagination. Is that true?"

"Yes."

He went on to explain that man was like the negative film upon which was printed the Image and Likeness of God. Just as the image in the camera was not clear until after the film had been developed, so the Image of God on the film of man's personality was not clear until after the personality had been through a similar process of development. In the meantime, it could be imagined.

"But," he continued, "since you know that God is love the whole matter is simplified. It becomes easy to imagine the qualities of love, and to grant that these are printed on the personality of Guard Peters, although you cannot see them. Your effort to see this God-Image in Peters is your developing process."

Under the old lifer's contagious inspiration, and the logic of his reasoning, I began to think of Peters in a far more kindly way. And as I thus thought of him analytically I could see that we had a great deal more in common than I had suspected.

We were both in prison; Peters as an employee of the state with a small salary, while I was a ward of the state with no salary. Peters was paid to serve time in prison to assure society that I served time in the same prison. Peters, little less a prisoner, guarded me, somewhat more of a prisoner. This guarding business I had resented.

Then it began to occur to me that, if seen in a different light, mine on the whole was the more fortunate position. It was true that Peters could go outside, while I had to remain inside. But, then, for this privilege, Peters had many responsibilities, while a benevolent state had generously lifted every social duty, obligation, and economic responsibility from my shoulders.

I was fed, sheltered, clothed by the state. I had no laundry or barber bills to meet. There were no insurance obligations to fall due, no lodge meetings to attend, or dues to pay. I had no rent, fuel, water, light, or doctor bills staring me in the face. I had no tax of any kind to pay, no local pride and civic spirit to maintain. And I had none of the annoyances incumbent upon the exercise of good citizenship, such as going to the polls on election day and of contributing to campaign funds and to other worthy causes.

Peters had a lot of these obligations, if not all of them. They were his price for being able to go outside. Their absence was my reward for having to remain inside.

On the other hand, Peters possessed many values that I did not possess; the love of a woman, and the subtle but large-looming joys of going home to one's family, the sense of honour and respectability, the touch of neighbours, and the possession of genuine friends who didn't fall away when trouble came near. The friends I had cultivated were repulsed by my troubles and were attracted to me only at times when my pockets were heavy with ill-gotten money.

As I reasoned thus the wall between Peters and me seemed to be melting away. Then I began to use my imagination in an effort to see in Peters that God-Image the lifer had told me to find. Slowly the list of God-qualities grew in my mind: love, truthfulness, integrity, sincerity, unselfishness, courtesy, thoughtfulness. On and on they piled up. And they were all latent in Peters, and they were all latent in me. They were printed on the film of our personalities. They represented that undeveloped Image of God in both of us. In these qualities, which were eternal, real, unalterable, Peters and I were one. Here we were not separated. Here no barrier existed between us. This was our common meeting ground.

So thrilled was I at reasoning and analysing my way to this enormous discovery and conviction of unity that my joy was uncontainable. It burst from me in tears of rapture. The lifer, understanding, became more concerned with his newspaper than he had previously been.

Guard Peters on his next round of the cellblock stopped at our door. He spoke to the lifer in his familiar tones of friendliness. Then, in exactly the same friendly manner, he greeted me unofficially for the first time in my life. This was almost too much. On top of the joy already bursting my soul asunder, this additional joy fairly made my head reel.

Not understanding, I thought of the incident as a miracle. There was no strain, no awkwardness or strangeness of any kind. It seemed the only natural thing for Peters to do. It was as though a wall had never been between us. It was as though we had always been good friends. I was included this time in the little chat. Now it was a three-way conversation. A short while before his arrival I had disliked Peters, and Peters had disliked me. When he moved on we were fast friends. A wall of Jericho had fallen.

I said to the lifer, "I wonder if you're thinking what I'm thinking?"

"It's not unlikely," he said. "Two guys locked in a little place like this are apt to chisel in on each other's thoughts."

"When Peters greeted me that way," I told him, "I couldn't have been more happy if it had been God Himself who spoke."

"Maybe it was God who greeted you," he suggested. "He uses His children to speak through. When the condition is made right and the instrument tuned in, He can use our voices, our eyes, our ears, our hands. Maybe it was God who spoke to you through the voice of Peters. Maybe, somehow, the conditions were made right."

I told him what I had done. "You know," I added, "before I had gone very far I had evoked a real feeling of affection for Peters. Does love always melt away the barrier?"

"Wherever love touches, a barrier goes down," he replied.

"The least important of these barriers are the objective ones. The main barriers to be removed are subjective, beneath the surface. That Peters made a concrete response to your feeling of affection is not the important thing. The important thing is that you evoked this feeling of affection and goodwill towards Peters. For this was your developing process. Peters, in this case, offered you your opportunity, *which brought out, momentarily, at least, the Image of God in you, so that what was revealed in you, you could see in him, and he could see in you,* although he did not then know what it was all about, perhaps. Are you happy about it all?"

My answer was a smile through a mist.

CHAPTER 12

RELAXATION

Be still and know that I am God: I will be exalted among the heathen, I will be exalted in the earth. —Psalm 46:10.

EARNING TO RELAX, MASTERING THE ART OF "LETTING GO," WAS a problem for me, who had lived for twenty-five years on the *qui vive*, like an animal, always alert to danger, sleeping fretfully with one eye open, as the saying goes, fearful of the law on the one hand—the guns of the underworld on the other. Suspense and intensity—these had been my life. Even at the time of my contact with the old lifer I still slept with taut nerves and muscles drawn tight for instant action.

"You must learn to limber up," the lifer said, "to pour yourself out, like a cat; to go limp, like a baby." He quoted the Master on the easiness of his yoke and the lightness of his burden. "There must be times of stillness," he continued. "God's voice is still and small. It can't reach you if your temples are throbbing and your pulses pounding. Stillness in you can soothe and calm the jangling nerves in others. Even the elements obeyed the quiet command of the Lord."

...and He said unto the sea, Peace, be still. And the wind ceased, and there was a great calm... And He said unto them, Why are ye so fearful? How is it that ye have no faith?

"It's important, son, that you learn how to let go. Learn to 'commune with your own heart,'" he quoted, "'upon your own bed, and be still.'" (Psalm 4:4.) And again from Psalm 139:18: "'When I awake,

I am still with thee.'" He added: "Learn how to enter sleep and you'll know how to wake."

And so the old lifer taught me how to relax. It was a night-time practice. The position was a reclining one. He went into some technical explanation in order to show me that nature herself was willing to assist me in my efforts.

"You see, son," he said, "the law of the earth is inertia. You have to keep the spine erect to overcome the earth's pull. When the spine is straight the currents which most play upon it are electrical. Like this..." He stood up, his spine perpendicular, and worked his fingers up and down rapidly to illustrate the activity of electrical vibrations. "Electrical currents induce action;" he went on, "magnetic currents, inaction."

He then informed me that when the spine was held in a horizontal position the currents playing upon it were predominantly magnetic. "And so," he finished, letting his neck and shoulders go limp, "when we recline or lie down we get drowsy. This is nature's way of helping us relax."

After the reclining position had been assumed, he then instructed me in the matter of emptying my lungs of stale air. Then I was to fix my attention on a dual process: on that of breathing and on the word *peace*.

Both the inbreath and the outbreath were to be slow and even and unrestrained. This was achieved by the will. The inbreath was to be shorter by several counts than the outbreath. A one-count pause was to be made at the end of the inbreath, and a two-count pause at the end of the outbreath.

I was assured that, while this was difficult at first, if persisted in, the particular rhythm would eventually establish itself and become a subconscious habit, thus eliminating the tedium of will control. On the slow-moving outbreath the word P-E-A-C-E was to be mentally and slowly pronounced.

It was amazing to see how this practice overcame tension and induced sleep and relaxation—a relaxation far deeper than that attained in ordinary sleep. And it eliminated subconscious activity in the form of dreams and restlessness. It produced a quality of restful slumber that can best be described as "peaceful." It was, in fact, and in a certain way, a spiritual experience with implications too far-reaching to suggest here.

In this experience of entering into peace at night, I have found the time element to be most bewildering. It is as though you drop off to sleep, and then wake suddenly a moment later. But the astonishing thing is that this moment has actually been a whole night. You're in the same position when you wake as you were when you dropped off to sleep. You apparently have not turned over and your body is so thoroughly relaxed that it may take a minute for it to respond to your will to move.

I am speaking here, of course, of my own experience. I do not presume to know just how proficient another may become in the practice of this particular method. But I do know that it has been a boon to me through the years. It has extended my working day, because four hours of this sort of sleep are more refreshing than a dozen hours of the half-conscious kind I used to know. From the practice of this method I have reaped a harvest of benefits in my physical, emotional, mental, and spiritual life.

CHAPTER 13

CONCENTRATION

...a double-minded man is unstable in all his ways.
—James 1:8.

INATTENTION, DIVIDED ATTENTION, SCATTERED ATTENTION IN plain words, double-mindedness and double-heartedness—was another enormous weakness in me.

As I said at the beginning, the lifer's ability to focus his attention on the thing at hand struck me as being an outstanding characteristic of the man. No matter what it happened to be, if it merited his interest he could fix his attention upon it instantly, and centralize all his energies around it. He could likewise shift his attention from it and back to it at will.

This ability to concentrate had given him a memory that was the talk of the prison. As for prison history, he was a veritable encyclopaedia. What he read he remembered accurately. The fairy tales and classic myths he could recite verbatim, ancient and modern history were open books to him. I have never met his equal in comparative religions, and it seemed to me that there was no subject he could not discuss with the knowledge and assurance of an authority. He had ranged over the field of philosophy and psychology, he was an expert theologian, and he had familiarized himself with all the best thought concerning the complicated subject of crime. Yet like Thomas Aquinas, when he came into a close personal experience of Christ, he pushed all the books on religion aside and devoted himself almost entirely to his Bible, and particularly the essays of Paul.

"You'll have to learn to concentrate, son," he told me, "if you expect to make a success in this life; if you want to have ears that can hear and eyes that can see."

He put the Bible before me and had me open it to the Book of Nehemiah before he began his lesson on concentration. As he told me to do, I read the 6th verse of chapter one, and I've never forgotten that line: "Let thine ear now be attentive, and thine eyes open, that thou mayest hear the prayer of thy servant."

He assured me that God's attention must be gained through our attention, a fact known well to the Psalmist when he sang: "Lord, hear my voice: let thine ears be attentive to the voice of my supplication."

As the old lifer taught me there are two fundamental methods for surrendering to the will of God. One of them is by way of single-minded attention on God and His Commandments, and the other is by way of relaxation, the opposite pole of action.

Psychology teaches us that our success in the world is due to our ability to organize our energies around the thing that we wish to accomplish. In other words, to be single-minded, to use concentration. For concentration fixes the attention upon the desired goal, and while the attention is thus focused our energy will flow in that direction.

"If concentration can give us worldly health and success," the lifer said, "isn't it logical to think it can give us spiritual success also?"

He did not immediately explain the various reasons behind his lesson on concentration. These reasons gradually dawned upon me, and then he discussed them from the vantage point of the results obtained. Primarily the lesson was an attack upon my sick- and double-mindedness. This was the way he explained it:

We lived in what Professor William James called "the stream of consciousness." Our minds, if we so willed, could operate as filters in this stream, or as a sort of clearing house, separating the good thoughts from the bad, and retaining the good and discarding the bad. The harm was not that bad thoughts entered our minds. The damage was done only by our being content to let such thoughts remain in our minds. Until a thought evoked and fused with feeling it had little power one way or the other over us. It was purely a matter of selection, the ability for which we possessed.

Until I could concentrate at will I should be the victim of the stream of consciousness and not its master. I should have no power of selection amounting to anything. Hence my mind would act as a retaining sponge for all manner of thoughts, good, bad, sick, and indifferent; my attention would be hopelessly scattered and I should be double-minded in all ways.

"That condition," he said, "is failure."

He presented two methods for correcting the condition of scattered attention. These were to be jointly employed until the desired result had been obtained.

The first method was to keep my mind so filled with spiritual thought that thought of a non-spiritual nature, when entering in, would be transformed into the image and likeness of that which resided in my habitual consciousness.

The other method was that of conscious will control, or of exercising my power of selectivity. This was to be in the nature of a game. It demanded close attention, like playing a game of chess. If, for instance, a negative thought entered my mind, I was not to give it attention, either by retaining it and reacting upon it, or by rejecting it with resentment. But I was to welcome it as an opportunity to counter immediately with two or more positive thoughts.

Within a few days I could readily observe the beneficial results of this latter practice. The old lifer assured me that any person, no matter to what depths of degradation he had sunk, no matter to what extent he had become victim to negative thinking, could change the whole course of his life by putting this method into practice for thirty days.

It is astonishing to note the rapidity of results when one buckles down in this unrestrained manner to take dominion over his thinking. It is essentially a method of *substitution*, rather than *rejection.* We are what we think we are, and when our thinking has been changed from negative to positive our whole life, including our environment, corresponds to the new order of things. But more astonishing is the fact that people are content to suffer defeat and all the miseries implied in the word when, with only a few weeks of earnest practice, their minds can be so reoriented as to overcome the destructive mental habits of a lifetime.

I have invented and practised a dozen or so methods of concentration effectively. None of these have been an improvement over those taught me by the lifer. I have tried the mental fast with varying results. But this is a rejection method, which, while effective, is still force. It is not the kingly way. It casts out thoughts it does not like. And where do they go when cast out? Right back into Professor James' stream of consciousness to be picked up and to victimize countless others. The lifer always had concern for the other fellow. So his ideal was not to cast out evil, but to transform it with the substitution of good. Every vice has its virtue and every virtue its vice. Hence he rejected nothing, but sought to release the virtue in everything, knowing that when the virtue had been thus extracted the vice would automatically cease to have existence. He used to remind me:

"Nothing has permanence but virtue. Nothing has impermanence but its opposite. Virtue is real. Vice is its shadow. Take the vice from the virtue and the virtue remains. The vice disappears. Take the virtue from the vice, and still the virtue remains, and the vice disappears." Hence his method of keeping the mind filled with spiritual thought, with virtue, with that which had permanence, eternal life, rather than with the shadows, which courted defeat and ended in death.

For what it may be worth I shall pass on to you a concrete example of concentration practice taught me by the lifer, representing one of the main features in this particular lesson. It has made concentration in other specific fields easier for me; and what it has done for me it will do for anyone else who is willing to persevere with a strong and earnest desire for improvement.

The lesson on relaxation was a night-time practice. The lesson on concentration was a morning practice. The objective of this latter practice was to make an actual conscious contact with God the first thing in the morning, so that I could be fairly certain of being sustained through the many harrowing temptations that swirl about the life of a convict every day. I am frank in saying, however, that I never could have persisted in this morning practice had it not been for the unimaginable patience of my old cell buddy.

The reason is this: the hour he set for me to practise was four a.m., at which time the pull of the earth is very great, and lassitude well-nigh unconquerable.

Had I been permitted to rise, stir about, or refresh myself, it would not have been so difficult. But right at this point the lifer was not interested in removing difficulties, but rather in arranging harder ones, saying, "The tougher the opposition, the more power must be released to overcome it." *Always he was interested in releasing my latent power.*

I soon learned to wake at the appointed time, but for quite a while the lifer had to prod me each morning before I would make the voluntary effort to keep my tryst with the God of morning.

It, too, was a bed practice. Upon waking I was not to get up, but merely to sit up, and put my mind on God as Love.

It sounds much easier than it is, for at this hour one can sleep with the greatest of ease. And a thousand reasons will crowd in to convince one that it is perfectly justifiable to turn over and drift away once more. When the earth is pulling you, as it does at that time, the intellectual mind can have small interest in looking Godward, and the personal will is far from being in a cooperative mood for this sort of effort. When you consider these mental and physical oppositions along with the more subtle urge to believe the whole thing as being fantastic and futile, you may well imagine that the practice is anything but easy. God could not afford to confine the heavenly approach to such a practice, for if He did I fear few of us would ever wind up in heaven.

But this I can say for those who have a flair for self-imposed discipline: a few weeks of persistence with this practice will be handsomely rewarded if, finally, the ability is gained to overcome inertia and keep the attention consciously fixed on the God of Love to the exclusion of all lesser thoughts. Even if the God-consciousness is not entered, the accomplishment is still a great mental victory with far-reaching values.

I still practise the method. It is no longer an effort with me. It has become a joyous habit. I'm not always successful in making the desired contact, but I do meet with more success than failure. The element of time and the factor of duty often interfere and thus determine success or failure. If given time enough success is almost certain.

Sometimes the vast serenity of the God-mind is entered within a few minutes. Sometimes it takes an hour, or even two. But, as I say, there are still other times when, though concentration is uninterrupted and easy, the experience is persistently deferred.

On those mornings when the God-mind is entered the effect throughout the day is like the running of spiritual tides. The mind is exceedingly clear and vigorous on those days. A large amount of work can be accomplished without mental weariness or physical fatigue. The appetite is good, digestion and assimilation are excellent. The heart seems to sing, and the time clock becomes an alien invention. There is a marked tendency, however, to consume too little water and breathe too little fresh air. I was advised to overcome this inclination by the exercise of will.

The lifer told me that the deeper one pressed into the world of the Spirit, the less desire one had for water. He claimed a connection between this fact and the Master's statement to the woman at the well that if one drank of the water which he possessed one would never thirst. However true that may be, my experience has been as stated above.

On the other hand, when the morning contact with God is not made the effect is often quite the opposite, with the result that the mental, emotional, and physical energies seem to flow at low tide. I have learned to operate on these days under the thought that in quietness and confidence shall come my strength.

Most of the people I have informed concerning this practice for the improvement of concentration have begun with enthusiasm, but to my knowledge only one has overcome the tug of inertia and wandering thoughts, to attain to direct and revelatory communion with the consciousness of God. But this one has become a skilled craftsman in the workshop of Christ. And if one more, because of reading this book, should achieve an equal capacity, the present chapter will have contributed greatly to the world's need, God.

The trouble is, perhaps, we haven't all an understanding friend who cares enough for our souls to tarry with us through the heartbreaking exasperations of the first few weeks, and who is willing to keep us prodded awake and persevering when it all seems so useless in comparison with the sweet sleep we could enjoy were it not for this tedious annoyance.

The Master was more considerate of his students than was the lifer. He told them to sleep on, justifying them on the ground that the spirit was willing though the flesh was weak. Sleep is a huge paradox: it makes what is sluggish seem light, and what is light seem sluggish.

I am glad that my old cell buddy was not so lenient with that weak flesh of mine. I am grateful that he kept it prodded until it could say to the spirit, "I, too, am willing."

CHAPTER 14

MEDITATION

I will meditate also of all thy work, and talk of thy doings.
—Psalm 77:12.

TO THE LIFER THE PSALMS WAS A BOOK OF MEDITATIONS. TO him meditation was an art, the greatest of the arts, because the least confined to conventional or standard forms. The purpose for meditation was threefold:

1. Meditation established a condition of consciousness which invited Revelation and the form best suited to its transmission.

2. Meditation established a protective atmosphere of reverence about a man which neither attracted familiarity nor an awkward reserve. It assured the mood of religion without imposing the danger of appearing religious. It left a man neither conspicuous nor inconspicuous. It warded off spiritual pride, and was a certain antidote against the disease of sanctimoniousness, and the folly of religious self-satisfaction. It placed one behind rather than in front of the Holy Spirit, and it courted health.

3. Meditation released the soul without imposing violence on the body or any of its attributes and faculties.

The subject for meditation, however, was all-important. The results obtained would correspond to the motive and the subject. If one meditated upon an invention, a painting, a play, for example, one would not produce something else, but would be likely to get increasing light on the particular subject of interest. If one meditated upon the subject of death and the spirit world, one would be apt to produce a psychic experience of some sort, or be drawn into a world of illusion so convincing as almost to appear real. If one meditated upon the question, "Who am I?" he would probably produce an experience of mental and emotional peace, a sort of Nirvanic state in which he seemed to take a holiday from life; quite pleasant, but holding dangerous possibilities for the weak and unstable temperament; a sort of exalted suicide, or a kind of mental hashish. If one meditated on an authoritative spiritual subject one would produce a corresponding experience of understanding. "I will meditate in thy precepts, and have respect unto thy ways." (Psalm 119:15). One is likely to have respect for that which he understands; one is apt to understand the precept upon which he meditates with purpose and earnestness. To meditate upon the passage, "The Lord is my Shepherd, I shall not want," is not likely to produce anything sensational or luminous; but one who meditates on this precept is likely to experience understanding and an enormous increase in one's faith.

The lifer did not seek to impose restrictions on my subjects for meditation, but he did want me to realize that there were different kinds of meditation, which produced corresponding results. He, himself, was highly proficient in the art of meditation.

As an art, available to all people, meditation is probably too little practised by our so-called busy population. To be too busy for the daily period of meditation is to miss one of life's sweetest delights and values. Five minutes in the meditative state is equal in value to a full hour's sleep. To me, man has invented no entertainment, no method for relaxation and pleasure that can remotely compare with the restfulness, the refreshment, and joyousness that is derived from meditation.

Meditation is also a secret for tapping Source Energy; that is, the energy of God. It is the great physical rejuvenator; the great emotional stabilizer; the great mental clarifier; and above all the great purifier of the accumulated negative habits that gather around and obscure the soul.

Meditation

Men who were as unlike as Edison and Immanuel Kant had developed the art of meditation to a high degree of proficiency. This may not have accounted for their long lives, but it certainly played an important part in the enormous amount of work they accomplished. We scan the mountain of work they left behind and our imagination reels at the thought of it. It seems inconceivable that anyone could achieve what either of these men achieved in the short space of a lifetime. They had each mastered the problem of personal efficiency by learning the art of "letting go" in the quiet of meditation.

The practice of meditation is especially helpful to men and women of large affairs and onerous responsibilities, and to those who find it necessary to burn the candle at both ends. As a spiritual technique, meditation is peculiarly fitted to business and professional people, and to those engaged in the arts and sciences. For meditation is the stage upon which these people can meet the world of religion in a spirit of oneness.

My public work has brought me into contact with business and professional people of all sorts. My observation has been that they are beset by a strange sort of hunger—a hunger for something satisfying to the heart and soul, which has not been found in any of the existing systems of religion. They seem starved for the Living Christ. Because they are more or less divorced from religious experience, because they are separated from the orthodox theological forms of religion and from the endless array of metaphysical interpretations, they imagine they are alien to any satisfactory religious ideal.

"I've found everything," said one man to me, "except the God you're talking about. Who is He? What is He? I'll be honest with you, I don't know what you people are driving at when you talk so freely of God. I sometimes wonder if you do. If He's what some religionists say He is, I want none of Him. They have nothing in their lives for me to envy. All I can see in them is confusion and war."

145

But he was hungry, nevertheless. Definitely agnostic, he had observed nothing in the practice of religion except that which had driven him farther toward a condition of atheistic scepticism. Together we worked out a meditation method for him. He caught on to the idea of "letting go," and was soon able to experience that for which he had hungered. Afterwards he exclaimed: "Why hasn't this been taught the world? Why?" His joy at finding himself had made him as naive as a child. He had come to life at last.

About the time of beginning my meditation practice I was employed in the prison shirt shop. The lifer suggested that my first efforts, therefore, should be aimed at a practical result: in this case, at the removal of occupational resistance, fatigue, and the slave-binding influences of time and place.

To illustrate what he meant by this he drew a comparison with the art of writing. He explained that much of the world's creative literature had been written under severe circumstances and trying external conditions. He pointed out that the creative writer often worked in cold and poorly ventilated rooms; that his position was often cramped, and in other ways physically exacting; that his diet was often unbalanced, his body inadequately exercised, and his eyesight unduly strained. Yet during the time he was in the glow of creation, the factors of time, place, and labour were all but unknown to him.

He declared bluntly that all these disadvantages were overcome by the transforming power of love.

"Where love is," he added, "there is an inner joy. And joy and the sense of bondage cannot exist together and be equally known."

He said that the former always absorbed the latter. The creative writer had a spontaneous love for his work. Loving it, he had joy in it, since joy was the nature of creative energy. And so long as his energy flowed in the direction of his work the strain of labour, the pressure of place, the slavery of time, were all removed from his immediate world.

Then I was informed that the creation of a shirt was as much a work of art and craftsmanship as the creation of a poem, if the attitude and approach were the same. *If I could make art out of my daily task I could accomplish it with the energy of joy. If I could release joy in my task I could overcome the pressure of the place in which I worked, the domination of time, and the stress and strain of labour. In other words, I could attain occupational emancipation by means of a meditative state of mind.*

It may be difficult to believe, but I did achieve this emancipation at my sewing machine by making an art of my work. I came to love my machine, and I knew that it loved me. To the uninformed it may seem odd, perhaps, to speak of a machine in love with its operator. But I'm sure there are men today with old cars who understand what I mean. Between the car and its owner there has grown up an indefinable affection. The old car has a language which the owner understands, special little squeaks which only he can define. They have been over the roads together, and always they have arrived. He wouldn't admit this strange love affair; but don't ask to buy his old car, for it's not for sale.

I learned to love my sewing machine, and it responded to my love. I'm not dealing here in fantasy. I'm dealing with facts. Between my machine and me a language was unfolded. It had a way of telling me what it needed, and the time came when it ceased to give me a moment's trouble. We were in love, and love generates harmony, order, co-operation—never discord and opposition.

My work became a game, and a joyous one. My aim was to make each succeeding garment better than the preceding one. I worked leisurely without lost motion, my fingers being guided into and around the flying needle with never an injury to them. I finished my task in less time than did the fastest operator in the shop, and my finished garments won the commendation of our shop superintendent, which was indeed a thing of rarity.

Having gone this far, I was ready for the next step, which was to bring the mind into a state of intentional dual action; that is, to carry on the mechanical and artistic work at hand, while at the same time keeping another part of the mind focused on Christ and all the ideas pertaining to him that came in and took form in this other section of my mental world. Though my food was poor, and shop conditions none too good, I had now overcome occupational fatigue and slavery, and thus I was prepared to make the shift of attention which I shall describe.

As I write these lines I am in the same sort of active meditation. My intellectual mind is busy with the mechanics of writing, and with those memories I am trying to convey; but my deeper mind is turning over many ideas concerning Christ and the purpose and meaning of his manifestation. It is the same dual process and may be employed with great benefit in any routine duty or activity to which the hand is called.

I shall give one example of this active meditational method. The actual examples of it in my own experience are numerous.

One morning shortly after we had taken our places in the shop, the empty space directly across from me was fitted up for a newcomer. Pretty soon a beardless, frightened and very naive youth was sitting in the chair facing a machine. Another prisoner, an old-offender, was instructing him. As he gave the young man advice along mechanical lines, he also advised him along the lines of "doing time." Not along the lines of "using time."

The youngster was impressionable and, as is usually the case with young first offenders, easily influenced by this first close contact with a fellow convict. He had come to prison with an assortment of ideals and good intentions. He would take advantage of his time, make a good prison record, and thus be ready to merit parole at the expiration of his minimum sentence.

It took the convict instructor about one hour to teach the boy how to operate the sewing machine. In the same hour he relieved the newcomer of all his ideals and good intentions. In their place he put the fundamental principles upon which the whole scheme of negative convict philosophy is based. The boy was informed that merit in prison was not rewarded; that all the favours went to the stool pigeons and official pets; that crime did pay if you worked in the big money; that the idea of social justice was an infantile delusion; that legal justice did not exist except in the minds of fools, and that no one ever got anywhere in prison by spineless submission, but only by hardboiled protest.

I sat across from this familiar scene and became aware for the first time that here was a subject for meditation, even though it was a subject so common that no one ever gave it a moment's attention. It was my opportunity to practise meditation upon the basis of what I had seen and heard. My first thought was that unless the miracle of spiritual experience entered in to check it, the newcomer was headed for the customary plunge downward and to a probable future of crime and prison punishment.

The Christ idea upon which I meditated took the form of questions. "With Christ an active power in prison, could such a conversation have taken place? Would this green, scared, and impressionable youth have been brought into direct contact with a man whose moral sensibilities had become entirely blunted and whose sense of responsibility no longer existed? With Christ as an active influence in the system of law enforcement, would the boy have been sent to prison where old and casehardened offenders were allowed to mingle with and influence susceptible first offenders? And with an acceptable and effective system of religion in operation in the prison, would it not have been possible to counteract the evil effects of this bad start which the boy got, or to have prevented that start?"

It took some four hours to complete my daily task. I did it without being overly conscious of time or place, and all the while I was preoccupied with the above-mentioned meditation.

This, therefore, is what I mean by active meditation. Right now, constantly in one part of my mind, I have a strong desire to be in meditation on God, while another part goes about the task of discharging the numerous routine duties of the everyday life. To express it differently, I have an aspiration to bring the glow of glory to the lesser things by keeping myself in the meditational mood concerning the greater things.

Over against this active method for meditation is its passive opposite. It is purely single-minded in its process and mystical in its result. It begins with relaxation, advances to concentration, and finally merges into meditation. The method demands a high degree of will control. The will fixes the intellectual mind quietly but steadily upon the idea of tranquillity until the effect willed is attained. At this point, through will again, the mind is fixed on Christ, or his equivalent, love, and is held there quietly but unwaveringly until the Revelations desired are attained. This method is what the lifer called the practice of the Presence.

After a while the personal will wearies of this lofty fixation. The effect is not that of an abdication of the personal will, but a complete and frictionless surrender of it. It is drawn in, so to speak, by the will of Christ or God. The intellectual mind is not thus absorbed, but, for the time being is purified, or cleared of all worldly confusion and speculation, and becomes a clear transparent medium through which Christ reveals himself, and wherein love, peace, and Reality are known. Many facets of the Christ gem are revealed in this experience, which are by way of interpretations of his cosmic character and mystical nature. However, the predominant effect upon the meditator is that of an unqualified and unspeakable love.

In this consciousness the highest form of healing may be practised by those who make the healing art a part of their spiritual ministry. It has, of course, many other utilitarian values. It takes away all doubt concerning eternal life; it gives a vibrant and boundless sense of security and fearlessness; and it bestows an enormous confidence in and dependence upon God for direction and supply. It leaves the mind washed and invigorated, the emotions peaceful, the body aglow with freshness and vitality. And it produces a general, all-round joyousness that can be described only as a zest for living to the fullest each passing minute of the day and night. It completely transforms the dream life, and gives one the capacity to sleep in the soft spiritual repose of a little child. Above all it makes Christ very near and dear, and the adventure with him the very highest kind of joy, serenity, and good pure fun. By assuring restful sleep it brings recovery and renewal at night, which proves a blessing during the daytime hours of work.

CHAPTER 15

CHRIST AS A QUESTION

Then said they all, Art thou then the Son of God? And he said
unto them, Ye say that I am.—Luke 22:70.

M Y EFFORTS TO PUSH BACK THE BORDERS OF A NEW LIFE
would have involved me in vast difficulties, had I not
learned to question every step of the way, not by the rule
of reason and analysis, but by *the rule of joy and adventure.* My natural
inclination has been to separate and analyse rather then to unify and
embrace, to work from the particular to the general, from effect to
cause, rather than from cause to effect. Had I been left to follow this
procedure, my recoveries along spiritual lines would have been
arrested long ago. But by counting all experience as adventure I have
been spared time after time from a too serious personal attitude
regarding the scriptural account of the Master's teachings.

On a dismal, fogbound morning with the prospects of a late
breakfast causing irritation to sweep through the cell house, I was
caught up in the contagion of useless rebellion, my soul seized with a
mood which demanded argument. I said to my cell buddy:

"There's something radically wrong with the concepts you hold
about Christ and some of the concepts in the Bible. These just don't
dovetail. You say that Christ is Love, unmodified and undefiled. The
Scriptures in many places show me a Christ who is everything but Love."

For half an hour he's been sitting on his stool before our cell door
coaxing sparrows from the corridor window with bits of bread.
There was one among them he called Thomas, another Peter, and a

third John. In answer to my remark he drew my attention to the birds on the window sill. Then he put another bit of bread on the cross bar of our cell door, and another piece on the stone step below. Immediately a little bird flew to the cross bar, perched there and pecked at the food, finally flying back to the window sill with the remainder of it.

"That was John," he said. "John is love, and love casts out fear."

By and by a second bird dashed across the corridor, took a hasty peck at the piece of bread on the step, and as hastily retreated.

"That was Peter," he said. "Peter is faith. But he isn't wholly convinced yet that he can depend upon God for protection. He's still a little fearful, nervous, hesitant, 'I believe in God, all right,' he says, 'but I'm taking no chances.' Faith needs a little of John's love to make him trustworthy and secure."

The third of the trio remained on the window sill, hopping back and forth in an undecided manner, very doubtful of the feast within his reach.

"That one is Thomas," said the lifer. "Thomas is reason. The bread of life lies before him in plain view. But it might be a trap. While he remains over there reasoning on the wisdom of possessing himself of this food, John or Peter will be back here and beat him to it. Oh, well, we'll go the other mile with Thomas." With this he tossed a piece of bread through the window, which the bird followed and captured.

"Oh," he recalled, "you were saying something about Christ. What was that again?"

I repeated the remark and added: "The Christ of the Scripture was intolerant towards everybody's religion but his own. He was hateful and bitter towards the Pharisees. Some of the language he used made him unworthy of my devotion, or even respect. It seems to me that your Christ has been sold down the river by some mighty poor translators. Looks to me as though he's lost in a bad arrangement of words and must be recaptured, if he's ever to be a high influence in my life."

"You might be right there," the old lifer agreed tentatively. "The true Christ is Love. And, of course, that's a state rather than a person. I guess Jesus is more the person of God, while Christ is more the state of God. Jesus might be the body of Love. Christ is Love. Maybe it was Jesus who condemned and Christ who forgave. The true Christ is Love, son. Now suppose Love has been rejected by the builders of theology, the creed-makers, and the translators. All well and good. But it holds a terrible temptation for you. If the true Christ of Love is to be recaptured from the debris of faulty translations, who is to do the recapturing?"

Since I could not trust myself to reply, he went on:

"You're to do it. You can study the Scripture until doomsday with your intellect, and the more you study the less you'll know of the message in it. Until you can bring to it the adventurous faith of our little bird, Peter, and the courageous love of our little bird, John, you'll have to remain on the outside window sill with our little bird, Thomas, and wait, in the doubtful hope that a crumb will be tossed to you. It is better to take the Scripture upon faith and love than to amend with reason that which eludes analysis."

Someone scraped his washpan across the bars.

"The men are becoming impatient for breakfast," he observed. "Men will heed the call of any empty stomach with an empty head. A hungry soul doesn't seem to matter much." He came back to the question under discussion:

"*You'll recapture Christ and know him by practising what he is. That's love.* There's nothing but disruptive force for you apart from love. Your only creative medium and unifying power in the world is love. Where love is there is harmony. Where it isn't there's discord. The controversial Christ is an unknown Saviour. Let others haggle over him. What has that to do with us? 'Follow thou me,'—here's the challenge. Christ is, always was, and ever will be Love. Everyone who proclaims him as less is judged by the Present, Past, and Future. All such are indicated by Time. On them the verdict of God is returned. Look well to your own course." He added:

"The controversial Christ is not your business, unless you want to make it so. The attention you give to such a Christ is little more than a so-called honourable excuse to avoid the issue of love. It might give you a way of escape which doesn't destroy your self-respect, or deplete your egotism. Regardless of how you read the Scripture, it will still reveal Christ as Love, Light, Life, and Law all bound up as one. He is the Lord, the Son of God, the Saviour, the Redeemer—and apart from these states there is nothing but confusion for you."

He looked at me intently for a moment, then declared:

"Christ is saying to you now—to you, remember; to you and you only, 'Whom say ye that I am?' And if you think you can answer that question with anything less than love, you may as well accept failure right now and quit tormenting yourself, for there's nothing but futility in store for you. There's no integrating power in this world but love. Because the hundred and twenty finally knew him as Love, they were able to go forth in love and gather in thousands of souls. A loveless sermon has never saved a soul and never will. And only by embracing and becoming love can you release your own soul."

I shall be eternally grateful to the lifer for his patience in making me see that Christ is not theology, philosophy, theory, speculation, argument, but is now and forever the sublime state of divine love, the stone that has been rejected at a horrible price to mankind, and that to recapture him from the ruins of rejection is a very personal problem, a very personal challenge, "Follow thou me."

CHAPTER 16

SURRENDER

...yield yourselves unto the Lord, and enter into his sanctuary.

WHEN THE LIFER DEALT WITH THE SUBJECT OF SURRENDER, as this word is used in a religious sense, he always thought of it as *yield*, which seemed to connote a readiness not quite apparent in the longer word.

"The harvest is not yielded up until it is ripe," he told me once. "Souls must be ripe unto the yield before they are ready to be garnered. To harvest an unripe soul would be like harvesting an unripe ear. The last estate would be worse than the first. The Holy Ghost could not be yielded up until the right moment had come. Neither can a soul be yielded up until it has been made ripe unto the harvest."

Surrender, he thought, could imply strain and force; while to yield implied an easy and spontaneous non-resistance, a giving up without effort, without any lingering restrictions or mental or emotional compromises, such as the young rich man had when the Lord offered him glory in return for himself, minus his holdings.

He thought it was a man's business to make himself ready, then the surrender would come as a yielding. It would be a real surrender, because the man would be transparent in it, his dark patches of pretence, self-deception, and exhibitionism would be gone.

Recently a group gathered in our home for a prayer and discussion meeting. It was a devastating test for the unready and timid, because, as it turned out, those present began individually to offer up prayer out loud. Personally I was not used to the method, and when my turn came I was all but mute. I stumbled about deplorably, grabbed recklessly at words, which had neither rhyme nor reason, and in general made out a bad case for myself before both God and man. I ended the ordeal as promptly as possible and took speedy refuge in the consoling thought that God was merciful and capable of making infinite allowances for me.

I felt no sense of timidity before God, but suddenly I had come under the grey blight before men. While my motives seemed all right, I nevertheless was not transparent. Something subtle and dark had emerged in me that was damaging to my influence, that got between me and my God, and between me and my fellows.

Later I found myself deep in the deception of self-justification. I found myself branding all vocal prayer as pharisaical, a form of exalted exhibitionism, and declaring to myself that silent prayer and meditation were the approved methods.

I was dealing in the old familiar alibi, and deep within me I knew it. I was not transparent even with myself. I was self-dishonest, untruthful, and insincere.

The man who was acting as the leader of the group made it bewilderingly simple. He was a man of many highly developed sides. He had been over all the philosophies, the theories, the systems. As a theologian he could have spoken with brilliance and impressiveness. As a philosopher he could have held us spellbound with the profundity of his knowledge and the vast range of his reading. As a scientist he could have caused our minds to swim with figures and symbols, with solar and cosmic mysteries. As a metaphysician he could have amazed us with the logic and diversity of his abstract interpretations. He was a man of academic attainment. He had hammered out many novels, books of non-fiction, plays, and magazine material. He had edited widely circulated magazines and periodicals. He had founded several.

The stage and screen had been among his mediums of expression. He could have impressed us all at this prayer meeting with the scope of his achievements. But the following constituted his instructions to us:

"Love is all there is. It all begins and ends here. Just surrender to the God of love in the best way you can. There's nothing else to it. Just let go. The word is love. The means, surrender. Give the problem to God, whatever it is. If we don't know how to surrender, let's give that to God, too."

No pretences, affectations, theatricals! No false mannerisms! Just simple, plain, honest, truthful, sincere, transparent! Being all this within himself, he was this with us. His vocal prayer was in keeping with his transparency. He didn't "formulate" it, or chisel it into something worthy of an English copybook. It, too, was simple, halting, hesitant, humble, unrehearsed. Much success and failure, much aspiration and spiritual vagabondage had brought him finally to this high, fine place—this loving, trustful, childlike faith and transparency.

My soul recognized his own soul's liberation and bowed to it. But for just an instant my intellectual self envied the man, though I was grateful for his leadership.

The problem of surrender was a favourite subject with the lifer. But he always implied that it held lots of disappointments and even tragedies for the unready and unaware. Like praying it could easily be done amiss. It could generate pride as well as humility, darkness as well as light, hate as well as love. It could leave scars and deep wounds. It could hurt as well as heal, degenerate as well as regenerate. The outcome of surrender was determined by readiness.

One time he asked me if I had ever seen a mountainside over which a forest fire had raged. Where once it had been stately and symmetrical, a personality adorned with majestic trees and verdure, it later revealed a great black scar, jagged, crooked, ugly.

"Fiery surrenders sometimes do this to you, son," he said. "The storms of spiritual conflict gather in and about the personality. They grow more violent and heated. Finally they reach a sort of crisis, and the tormented victim rushes in blindly where wise men fear to tread." With measured deliberation he added:

"Because of their impure bodies, unready for the spiritual fire, unprepared for the purgatorial, divine holocaust to rage through them, there is a thousand times more burning than purging. And the little gained is rarely worth the ravages invited."

According to the lifer the urge to surrender should come as the natural result of preparedness and spiritual aspiration, and not as the result of whipped up emotions, fear, and frustration, the negative desire to escape evil, rather than the positive desire to embrace good.

I have never made a complete and unconditional surrender, because in the first place I do not believe it possible. When a man's last secret sin has been yielded there is no need for him to remain in the body. His accomplishment here has ended. I was warned against this constant temptation to declare an unconditional surrender for myself. I was taught to move steadily towards the surrendered life, while recognizing my limitations all the way. Hence I have been obliged to take my moments of surrender piecemeal and without violence. In this manner certain flaws in my character have vanished without my knowing when or how the change took place. Many undesirable habits have gone without leaving behind them a single trace of scar-tissue. Many other undesirable habits and flaws persist. I pay little if any attention to them. Instead, I continue my aspiration God-ward, not because of my unwanted habits; but in spite of them, and because I find it more fun and adventure to aspire God-ward.

Of course, self-examination and self-inquiry are among the interesting features of this adventure. It is interesting to lose old habits without knowing when they took leave. It is interesting to observe results as they occur in my experience, and to compare them with similar results in the experience of others.

In one man's experience the habit of fear had been overcome, and he was engaged in teaching others how to overcome their fears. When I am in the love-consciousness I am entirely fearless, but I am not always in the love-consciousness. There are those who can testify to this fact. On the other hand, I can truthfully say that most of the fears have passed from my voluntary sense-consciousness, but there is still an involuntary sense-consciousness with which I have to deal. This is quite a different matter. I have observed that the cells in my body can be afraid when fear seems entirely absent from my mind. This fear has been implanted in my cells through incredible ages of race fear, ignorance, and superstition. In my mind I know these cell fears are illogical and unreasonable, but this knowledge does not banish the fears. In the presence of the weird, the unknown, I am still capable of gooseflesh, of cells gone panicky along my spine, even though my mind proclaims heroically that there is nothing to fear.

Consequently I am inclined to be moderate when I set out to teach others how to rid themselves of fear, though I shall probably continue to do so. I have a feeling that all people should be freed of the bondage of fear, and I have tried to inform some of them on the subject. I am sure I have never been wholly convincing, however, because of my doubtful authority to speak along this line. It has occurred to me, on the other hand, that fear might be the very thing they need as a compelling drive in their lives towards the foot of the cross. I have felt often that it might be better just to turn them over to God, who knows best what they need, and how best to supply it.

Another man in his experience of surrender had lost a physical habit, that of drink. But in its place he had gained a mental habit, that of intolerance. He now attacks the drink habit in others with undisguised fury. He hates people who drink, and he lives in mortal fear of liquor himself. It is a constant temptation to him. His surrender has brought a penalty to balance a profit.

I had been a confirmed drunkard for many years. I had loved not only the effects of liquor, but the taste of it. The desire for it has vanished from my life. I don't know when or how. Liquor has no temptation for me, and I do not in the slightest degree fear it. Nor do I hate those who indulge in it.

The ingrained habit of crime has left me completely. It has positively no lure, no temptation for me any more. I do not in the least fear it, and I do not hate those still subject to its bondage. I work with scores of criminals in a private way, and I have no desire whatever to change a single one of them. That is God's business, and so far as I am concerned, no power less than God's can banish the thoroughly conditioned habit of crime. I have a desire to share my experience with them, providing they want to share it. They are my friends, indeed, when they make it possible for me to share with them those values which I have realized. My attitude in the matter, therefore, is that they furnish me with the chance to further my own growth.

But I have met several ex-convict evangelists who have surrendered their criminal personalities and who now insist that all other criminals emulate their example. And I am afraid their insistence can but invoke disgust and an equally robust resistance on the part of the criminals they would reform.

Crime to these fellows is a constant below-the-surface temptation. They fear it, and they are intolerant towards those who are still victims to it. They have surrendered one vice to gain another. The exchange is questionable for them, though fortunate for society, perhaps.

I repeat that these analyses and comparisons are most interesting and plainly indicate that there are at least two fundamental approaches to the problem of surrender: the one by love and non-resistance, returning good for evil; the other by hate and warlike resistance, attacking evil with evil. Jesus Christ and the future are on the side of the first proposition.

A thousand times during these past ten years I have been tempted to surrender wrongly, to yield to impatience with my progress and the tenacity of certain personality faults and habits, and to set upon them with storm and war, determined by the exercise of my own will to drive them out of my orbit. But always before I am ready to carry out this notion, I hear once more the calm voice of my old cell buddy:

"Take it easy now, son. Don't get yourself all flustrated. Rome wasn't built in a day, and the Universe is still young. There's no end. Just a steady growth. Keep reaching towards the Kingdom and illumination will come. In its gently falling light old barriers will depart in the right way and at the right time. There'll be no sores left to fester and itch. *When the surrender is right, God always gives a virtue for your vice.*"

One of my undesirable habits is an embarrassing sense of timidity, which rises when I least want it. On the public platform this habit often causes me to teach instead of *be*. It impels me to manufacture my discourse in advance, thus corroding my faith in God. Worse still, it causes me to drag along a handful of notes just in case I shall need a crutch to support me in some sterile interlude. It often prevents me from going before my audience empty of preconceived notions and opinions, and from trusting the Spirit to say the right thing through me at the right time and for the right person out there. In short, it causes me to get in the way, to strut out in front of God, instead of lingering in the background open, free, and usable. It causes me to be like the preacher who forgot his notes one Sunday morning and was forced to make the following apology to his congregation: "Ladies and gentlemen, in my haste to get here this morning I came away without my notes. Consequently I shall have to rely entirely upon the Lord this morning. I can assure you, however, at the evening service I shall come better prepared."

I quietly surrender this problem—and wait. In the meantime I shall continue to adventure. Aspiration goes on.

CHAPTER 17

HEALING

B Y THE COMBINED EFFORTS OF MEDICAL SCIENCE, MENTAL science, and spiritual science I was healed of many dangerous bodily afflictions. In the process of being healed I learned, through observation, many valuable lessons concerning the art of healing. The greatest of these lessons centred in the word *cooperation*. When the medical, mental, and spiritual practitioners work together the healing miracles of Jesus are placed within the orbit of a suffering humanity.

The foundation of the healing art is an alert and growing medical science. Just as a community without a church runs towards lawlessness and ruin, so would the healing art without a medical science become a wilderness of quackery and murderous experiment and practice. Medical science must ever be the watchdog as well as the minister in a world of sickness and sin.

But medical science should not assume that it represents the whole of the healing art. Nor should mental and spiritual science make hasty and irrational claims of independence.

Three chances are given to men. A man can deny God the Father. He still has the chance of affirming God the Son. A man can deny God the Son. He still has the chance of affirming God the Holy Spirit. But if a man deny God the Holy Spirit he has committed the Unpardonable Sin by virtue of the fact that he has denied his third and last chance for salvation. There is then but one direction for him to follow, and it will inevitably lead towards intellectual futility and spiritual sterility.

If a man is ill he may seek the aid of a medical doctor. If before his condition the skill of medical science stands helpless, he may turn to mental science for relief. If in mental science he can find no hope, there is still the spiritual practitioner to whom he can make his appeal. All are healing branches operating on different levels of the same Divine Art.

The heroism in the healing art is found chiefly in medical science. It is the medical scientist who is first on the job in times of flood, epidemic, and great territorial disaster. It is the medical scientist who takes the great risks and who makes the great personal sacrifices for the healing art.

The education in the healing art is found chiefly in mental science. It is the mental scientist who probes deeply into the causes for disease and establishes the modes of conduct for its elimination.

The great spiritual values in the healing art are released through the spiritual healers. Such a healing tends to reinforce faith, and it often changes the whole course of life for the one who has thus been healed. Many of the great Christian organizations can trace their inception to the healings of their founders. When health has been restored through personal or intercessory prayer, there is nearly always a strong impulse thereafter to render one's health to God in some sort of spiritual service.

This has been my experience.

The series of teachings presented in the preceding chapters were all given while I occupied a cell with the lifer and while I was undergoing a process of healing in my own body parts.

I was in the best of health on the day I had an unexpected interview with the warden. The position of night nurse in the prison hospital was soon to be open. I was told of the responsibility this position carried. It was the most responsible post within the reach of any convict. And to him who assumed it went the maximum of official trust. Here the trusted convict had to do nothing that went against his honour, such as giving information against his fellows or performing other unsavoury acts in return for official favours. The job demanded the last ounce of the convict's active and potential honour and integrity.

What a strange position to be offered me—the man who had almost killed himself in a vain effort to get a sick bed in the prison hospital. The offer stunned me and sent me back to my cell bewildered and dizzy with the mystery of it.

"It's no mystery, son," the old lifer assured me. "It would be a mystery if you hadn't been called upon to take this job. You're now equipped for it. It belongs to you. The warden isn't sending you to the hospital. God is doing it. You'll have access to things that would be dynamite in the hands of the untrustworthy, and you'll have also endless opportunities to practise God's presence through the sick and suffering bodies of His most misguided children. Let love go before you. You follow. It will be revealed what you shall do in a given case."

I found the hospital honeycombed with petty intrigue, childish jealousies, and departmental frictions. As in other departments of the prison, convicts were vying with one another for favour and prestige, for official notice and commendation. Plots and counterplots were prevalent among the convict attendants. Lies against one another were hatched up and peddled to the warder and doctor. Into this I went with the lifer's final advice ringing in my ears: "Your only obligation is to love nobly and well. Take no sides. Make friends of all, but have no special friend or friends. Then you'll be about your Father's business. Take sides ever so slightly, and you're lost."

Months later I had the opportunity to repeat this wise advice to a new night warder. He failed to heed it. And he was lost. When he came on duty that first night, with tears in his eyes, he told me what this job meant to him. For eighteen months he had been unemployed. His wife and four children had been subjected to penury. His suffering as the willing but helpless provider had been bitter and intense. At the blackest point, it seemed, in his life a miracle happened.

A friend appeared who had influence in the state government, a job as guard in the prison was offered, he qualified, and was hired.

"I want to keep this job," he added. "If ever a man needed it that man is me."

"It's one of the best of the guard jobs, Cap," I reminded him. "And it's the hardest job in the place to keep. You're here, a green man, because the warden is tired of putting promoted men in here only to find them incapable of dealing with this situation a few weeks later. The old-timers all know too much for this place. If you get started right you've got a chance to make the grade. I can help you if you want my advice."

He assured me that he would be most grateful for anything I could suggest that would help him hold the job down and make good on it.

"Men in prison have to have pastimes," I began, "something to interrupt the monotony of sameness and time. So they often invent ways to overcome the pull of dullness. Here in the hospital they plot against each other and, if possible, against the warders. Even the doctor must be on his guard against lies and schemes. For some of them, on the surface, look mighty genuine and have been spun from clever and practised minds. Whatever you do, Cap," I finished, "don't take sides with one group in here against another. And don't believe very much what you hear. And be cautious even of some of the things you see. If you're smart you can hold your job and keep bread on your family's table."

This advice was received with thankfulness. I felt rather good about it, for in the practice of healing prevention was worth more than cure. I liked the new warder, which was an asset since I was the one who had to work with him night after night. Understanding cooperation between us meant smoothness and effectiveness. And after hearing his story, I had a deep desire to see him make good and hold his job for his own and his family's sake.

However, he was too easily swayed. He lacked the necessary experience and sophistication. He was trapped by the very thing I had warned him against. The irony of circumstances would have it that I was used to bring about his undoing. I reasoned with him. I tried to persuade him. I prayed for him. I even tried to enlist the aid of the lifer's prayers. But he had only this reply:

"God had given the warder the power and intelligence to do his job over there, and to do it well. If he does not care to use the gifts of God, then he'll have to look to a sterner guide, experience."

At night my duties often took me to the hospital kitchen. Without my knowing it, a jar of prunes in some sugared water had been secreted in one of the pantries, where the mixture was allowed to ferment. Then someone quietly informed the warder of its where-abouts, gave me as its owner, and said that I was taking advantage of my position to make intoxicating liquor. The warder investigated and discovered the incriminating evidence. With a grave face he con-fronted me with his proof. He was terribly sorry that this had to happen.

"But there's only one thing I can do," he finished. "My duty."

And from this conviction he could not be moved. He made out a written and signed report against me and sent it to the deputy warden.

On the day of prison court I found myself waiting with the large group of accused men assembled in the room behind the Yard Office. It so happened that on this day the state surgeon was to be at the prison for four major operations. My duty in this connection was to have everything sterilized and in readiness. Having anticipated the interference, I had made all the preparations in advance. When the surgeon arrived at the hospital he found everything ready and in its proper place but me. Impatiently he inquired for me and was told what had happened. When he arrived in the Yard Office he was in a slashing mood.

I was called in to face my accuser. The deputy read the report and asked the warder if it bore his signature. He confirmed the fact. I was then asked concerning my guilt. I denied the charge. For this very same act of denial months before I had been thrown into the hole. Now I was asked if I had anything to say in support of my denial.

"I'll do that for him," the surgeon spoke up. Then turning to the warder, he asked, "What keys do you carry when you're on duty at night?"

"No keys," was the reply.

"And what keys do you carry?" He now addressed the question to me.

"I have a key to the dispensary, and all medicine cabinets," I replied.

"You go in and out of the dispensary at will?" he next asked.

I nodded.

"What is kept in that dispensary?"

"Supplies," I answered.

"Any liquor in there? Any grain alcohol? Any narcotics?"

I admitted that considerable quantities of these were kept in stock.

"Ever sample any of it?" he asked.

"No," I said.

"You could have, couldn't you?"

"Yes," I replied.

"But you prefer to drink mouldy, poisoned prune juice to good liquor." He turned to the deputy. "I'm operating in twenty minutes," he said. "You'd better stick your warder in the hole on a charge of indefensible stupidity, while I put your convict to work."

I explained to the deputy exactly how the thing had happened, and I recounted the warder's story as he had told it to me. This frank recital I am certain saved the man his job, though it cost him his place in the hospital. The experience was a good teacher, and he became a well-balanced and efficient prison guard.

CHRISTIAN HEALING

On an evening some weeks before I had entered upon my duties as night nurse, our cell had been quiet for an hour, save for the occasional rustle of my newspaper. The lifer had been almost breathless with a novelette in an old mystery story magazine, which I had brought in that noon.

"Say, old timer," I asked, interrupting him shamelessly, "is Christian healing Christian?"

He grunted an affirmative and continued his reading.

"Not according to this piece in the paper," I replied. "Here's a minister who doesn't believe in it."

The old lifer's magazine was instantly abandoned and he was on his feet. "You're to go by the Bible," he snapped. "There are at least sixty references to healing in the Old Testament, and seventy-five or eighty in the New. Healing's as much a ministry as preaching."

He called for the Book. Vigorously he turned the pages and put his finger on the 6th verse of chapter 9 according to the Gospel of St. Luke. "What does that say?" he asked. I read:

And they departed, and went through the towns, preaching the gospel and healing everywhere.

"Turn back now to 6:19," he prompted. I read the passage:

And the whole multitude sought to touch him: for there went virtue out of him, and healed them all.

"Does this tell you anything?" he asked. "You see in this last passage that he set the example, which was followed by his disciples as recorded in the first passage. What you read there in that paper is some man's opinion. What you read here in this Book is history and authority."

Through this incident I was led into a new field of spiritual practice, Christian healing as a means of practising the Invisible Presence of God.

My interest in the subject, I am sure, had much to do with obtaining the job in the prison hospital. In this position I was able to observe at first hand scores of healings effected by supernatural rather than by natural means. I came to believe that Christ and his disciples were able to heal all manner of disease, the truly organic as well as those of hysterical origin. I came to believe also that modern disciples of Christ would be raised up who could do likewise, men and women with power sufficient to effect cures even in cases where the cause was genuinely organic.

The lifer doubted a large percentage of such causes.

It was his opinion that most of the known diseases could be traced to mental and emotional states in the individuals or their families, or to the negative collective thought in nations and races. He believed, for instance, that pernicious germs were the products of men's pernicious thinking, and that a germ disease could not be permanently healed by destroying the germ's form; but by correcting the cause out of which the form came to be. So long as the cause remained it would produce another and probably different form, and thus give us another and different epidemic of contagion.

In short, the old lifer sought to sell to me the idea that nearly all the cases I would meet with had behind them an origin of some kind of hysteria. With all due allowance for another opinion, my own experience has inclined me toward his view. This will be my position particularly throughout this chapter.

On a hospital bed a man lay dying. His mother, poorly clad and marred frightfully by the ragged edges of life, by self-denial, scrimping and scraping, had accumulated enough money to pay her son a visit, which she thought would be her last opportunity to see him in this life. She said she had walked part of the way. How she was to get back home she did not know. She was at her son's bedside. That was enough.

No one knew just why he did it, nor did he know himself, but the orderly in the ward entered the room with a full-page picture of the Crucifixion scene, which depicted the Triumphant Christ departing

172

from the limp and heavy body hanging on the cross. He had torn this picture from a Sunday newspaper Supplement. He was surely not what one would call a religious man. On the surface, at least, he was profane and often vulgar. Without speaking he spread the picture across the sick man's bed and directly under the old mother's eyes. Then he withdrew, and disobeyed the rules by closing the door behind him. Quietly he took up his duties.

The guard passed along, scrutinized the closed door, and went on. The doctor came into the ward, looked toward the closed door, and stepped back into the elevator. The regulation half hour allowed to visitors passed. Apparently no one in official charge knew that the time was up for the dying man's mother. The convict attendants passed to and fro softly. An hour went by, and then two. Three hours had elapsed when the mother emerged of her own accord. In her hand she clutched the picture. Her eyes were wet, but there was a light in them that had not been there before. Another patient called it a light of faith. The tired lines that had been on her face were less obvious, because of a certain glow that had come to her.

A man by the name of "Pickhandle Charlie," a giant of a fellow, and dangerous, who was in the hospital recovering from a knife wound he had received in a fight, went up to the old lady and inquired about her son.

"He'll soon be well now," she affirmed. "We prayed together, and God answered our prayer. I felt it inside of me when He did it."

"Us boys out in the convalescent room prayed, too," Pickhandle Charlie told her. "We know Ed'll get well now. We had a fight once, Ed'n me. There was bad blood between us. I held a grudge against him. That's all gone now. We made up a little gift for you. Not much, but it'll getcha back home, and there'll be some over."

This patient, according to sound medical judgment, should have died. But he didn't. What is more, his recovery seemed to occasion no surprise to anyone. He was healed of his physical affliction, but better still he was healed in his moral parts at the same time, later to leave prison and become a blessing to his believing and sacrificing mother.

A young convict was brought into the hospital on the verge of a nervous breakdown. He recovered slowly. However, as he gained in physical strength, his eyesight seemed to fail, until, by the time he was healed in the other parts, he was blind.

There followed several weeks of what I like to call spiritual re-education. Methods conveyed to me by the lifer were applied to the patient. When the old lifer considered the lad sufficiently prepared, he handed me a small copper disk, which he himself had made. On one side he had engraved the word "Light," on the other side the word "Love." Then he instructed me carefully as to just what to do with the object.

First I was to talk to the boy about it until his curiosity was thoroughly aroused Then more talk until his interest in the object had greatly increased. Finally I was to tell him that on this disk were two magic words which embodied all the healing power there ever was or ever would be. Immediately he wanted to know what the words were. This information was withheld. A compromise was made.

"At nine o'clock tonight," I told him, "I'll put this charm with its magic words in your hand, and if you want to know what the words are, and you want to know it strongly enough, your eyesight will be restored and you'll get to see the words for yourself."

The patient went to sleep with the disc in his hand. He had an exciting dream in which he and the object were intimately involved. It seemed that he was alone in a boat far out in the middle of a large lake. He was standing up in the boat and flipping the disc in the air, catching it as it came down. The boat tipped and both he and the disc went overboard. It was just out of his reach going down. He kept after it, diving, diving, reaching and straining, until the pressure on his lungs suddenly sent him into a panic of fear. He woke clutching desperately the piece of metal in his palm. There was perspiration on his face.

His eyes had regained their sight.

His scream brought me running to his side. A moment later the light was put on and he looked upon the two magic words.

Psychological blindness! Yes, indeed! But blindness just the same!

"Was this not a trick?" I asked the lifer. "Would you call this Christian healing?"

His answer was a passage in the Bible where Jesus made mud of spittle and told the blind man to wash it off his eyes.

"Do you s'pose that mud had healing power, son," he asked, "or was it the Master's power of suggestion which did the work? Do you think the metal disc had healing power, or was it your power of suggestion which did the work?" The old lifer smiled as though he were deeply happy over this outcome.

"It's a good piece of work," he said.

To the prison came a promising fellow of twenty-two. He came highly recommended, and was in line for a clerical job just as soon as he had served the three months necessary to place him in the first grade. This initiation period was usually spent in what was called the "fish" gang, all of its members being newcomers, except a few old-timers who acted as "runners," water boys, tool-tenders, and the like.

On his first day's assignment to quarry duty he was told by one of the old-timers, who was a practical joker, that just as soon as he made first grade he would be transferred to the overall shop. Then he was told what a horrible place that was. The tasks were impossible. Strong men went crazy in that shop. Some had been known to cut their right hand off in order to get out of it.

Late that night the fellow was brought to the hospital. He was shaking as though he had the chills, and his right arm hung limp at his side.

The warden was quite disturbed about the case, due to a certain political influence that was back of the man through his parents. It was

175

more than just another hospital case. It was a situation, and the warden was insistent that something be done about it as soon as possible.

The doctor's diagnosis was based upon a physical rather than a psychological examination, and the result was mystification. Treatment proved wholly ineffectual, and the doctor, too, became alarmed.

The lifer advised me to make friends with the patient, gain his confidence by sharing with him some secret knowledge of my own, and then begin a close and indirect examination of the fellow's emotional reactions from the first day he entered prison. This method revealed the above-mentioned information, and laid bare the psychological cause for his apparent paralysis. He had brooded over the possibility of being assigned to the overall shop. The suggestion that an amputated hand supplied the means of escape from this terrible fate had sunk deeply into his subconscious mind. In the night it did its work. It could not realize for him a severed hand, but it could achieve the next best thing, a lifeless and useless one.

The treatment in this case was taken out of the doctor's hands, and was placed in the warden's. When the patient was assured that a clerical job was waiting for him just as soon as he could operate a typewriter, the arm was almost immediately restored to normal.

Hysterical paralysis! Yes, indeed! But paralysis just the same!

Years ago, many years ago, as a boy wanderer and derelict along the Mexican border, I came out of a comatose state following an extended bout with poor liquor. I was lying on the only bed in a small shack. The first thing upon which my eyes fell, after I became conscious, was a Mexican woman, her eyes closed, her lips moving in prayer. She was kneeling with her face toward a small shelf on which was a picture of the miracle-working Saint Jude. A little boy was at play outside the shack.

I had staggered to her door and collapsed. What her prayers had to do with my healing I do not presume to know. I only know that I was ragged and filthy and critically ill, a drunken sot and vagabond, and that she had received me, put me on her only bed, and prayed for my recovery. But I have come to believe in the efficacy of a righteous person's prayers, and she was righteous.

I walked away from her to render my recovered health to Satan. Whatever the source of this healing, it had not reached my moral life. However, God does work in a mysterious way His wonders to perform. The years fell one by one into the cesspool of crime and dissipation, and I had come to my last prison hitch and my last prison job: night nurse.

Then to the hospital one night came a Mexican youth. His age? About my age at the time I was healed below the border. The doctor's verdict? "The will to live is gone in him."

The youth could not speak English. He was far from home, just another victim to the scourge of prison grief. He had doomed himself with his own mind. Weakened through loneliness, shame, and despair, he fell prey to a deadly abdominal ailment, for which he had had a pre-disposition.

I went to his bedside. His large, pain-rimmed and bewildered dark eyes lifted to mine. They were hollow, feverish, and terribly homesick eyes. As I looked into them I remembered two things. One thing the lifer had said just before I entered upon my duties in the prison hospital, *"Put love in your eyes and let them look at it."* The other thing I remembered was a Mexican woman kneeling beside my sick bed years before, her own boy playing just outside the door.

From our visiting priest I secured a picture of Saint Jude. This I placed on the table at the foot of the patient's bed. I was not of the Catholic faith, but the young man was. I joined my non-denominational faith with that of his ancestors. And I kept the vigil. I knelt just as the Mexican woman had knelt, and my petition was offered up with my face toward the picture.

Whether or not there was any healing virtue in this ceremonial observance, I have no notion whatever. I only know that it helped to focus my mood and to give me a single-pointed attention.

I have a very decided conviction that love is the healing energy, and that energy follows attention. The more fixed the attention the less scattered the energy!

My love for the Mexican youth was spontaneous. I am convinced that this love could never have effected a healing in him, because it was purely human and therefore of a possessive nature. But when my love was lifted to God through the medium of the Saint, the possessive quality in it was transferred. From a personal possession of the boy the order was reversed to become a possession of him by God.

The healing was effected, and what had been a rapid decline toward death became a rapid ascent toward health, and finally a complete recovery.

There may be little value in the abstract speculation upon this healing, but since I present the case and make the bold assertion that it is the energy of love which heals, the reader has the right to know about my analysis, faulty as it may be.

"If love heals," you may argue, "why is not every sick person healed, since there is someone who loves him and desires his healing?"

My answer to that is that it is not the selfish, personal, possessive love which heals, but the reversal of this love which effects the healing. Or as Professor Glenn Clark has pointed out: "The healing takes place at the point where we relinquish the person we love." *In other words, when we are willing to give our loved one away to God, without compromise or qualification, God in turn, if it be His will, is apt to give the loved one back to us.*

Purely human and possessive love does not trust God. When the loved one is menaced with danger or is afflicted with a deadly disease, human love is inverted into the energy of fear and anxiety, which is a destructive and not a constructive or healing energy. It is, however, energy. And it is the energy, though negative, which heals when it follows attention that is not focused amiss.

Healing

As an example of this I could cite a number of cases out of my own experience. I shall present one, the case of my stepdaughter. At one period in her childhood she became dangerously ill. Both her mother's and my love for her being purely human and possessive, it promptly began to manifest itself in us as fear and anxiety. I held the child in my arms, shifted with great difficulty my attention from her to God, and upon Him kept my attention fixed.

Gradually an alteration in my feelings began to take place. The heavy weight of anxiety began to lighten, as though it were being lifted up. As this proceeded, the anxiety seemed to be correspondingly replaced by a feeling of greater trust and assurance. This feeling steadily grew, until eventually there was a point reached in my consciousness which can best be described as a complete yielding to God's will in the matter. I knew then, both by thought and feeling, that this child belonged to Him and not to us, and that He alone knew what was best for her. Thus, not by mere lip action, but by a spontaneous act of surrender, our possession of the child was released, and she was given into the possession of God.

His answer to this was a feeling of serenity in me, a great inner rejoicing and an all-consuming emotion of gratitude. Instantly the child's fever vanished, she opened her eyes, said she was hungry, and, after being fed, she was placed into bed where she slept soundly all night. She awoke in the morning completely restored to her normal good health.

ABSENT TREATMENT

My personal opinion is that both mental and spiritual healing transcends the three-dimensional plane and enters the fourth. In regard to the psychiatrist, I am certain that a majority of the cases treated by him could more effectively be treated if his own personality were kept away from his patient. Persons suffering from mental and nervous disorders are hypersensitive; they are easily repulsed and easily attracted by the forces operating in the personality of another.

The professional air of the practitioner may be attractive and beneficial to one patient and wholly repulsive and destructive to another. His animal magnetism may work against him in certain patients by arousing adverse feelings. By this play and interplay of forces one patient may be repelled, while another may be wooed into harmful displays of exhibitionism.

If the mental healer could accept the idea of absent treatment upon a basis of faith, if not reason, I feel sure his cures would mount on the side of those patients who are defeated by the forces in his personality when these are contacted at close range.

Jesus, the Master Healer, employed both psychiatrical methods. To some He presented His personality and asked questions and gave suggestions. Again He preferred the absent treatment and "sent His word and healed them," which was an early example of healing with a method now employed by many mental healers who prefer telepathic treatment to the personal interview type. All treatment is experimental, faulty, and often dangerous, except that done by the direct intervention of God Himself, for only God can interfere with an individual's will with impunity.

My wife was carrying on a little visiting ministry in one of our large local hospitals. One day she came upon a most pathetic case of a young woman in the final stages of cancer. That morning reflex tests had been made and the woman was found to be paralysed from the waist down. Upon inquiry the attending physician informed my wife that the patient had only a week or two at most to live.

This information and story was repeated to me when my wife returned home. At the fatal verdict of medical science there seemed to well up within me a huge, uncompromising "NO." I went to a hammock in our back yard, made a mental identification with the patient, and began to think of her in terms of health. My meditation lasted an hour. Then suddenly I felt an unalterable sense of assurance. I went into the house and said to my wife, "It has been done." I had not told her of my intention to treat the woman. "What has been done?" she asked. "The woman with the cancer," I replied. "She has just been healed."

This patient was discharged to a rest home two weeks later. My wife in checking with her on the exact time of her healing found it to be as I had stated. The woman described it as "A great inrushing of new life, followed by the ability to move the lower part of my body." Her recovery was gradual, but complete within six weeks after she had entered the rest home.

SOME FURTHER EXAMPLES

Psychological. There was a convict for whom I could evoke only a modicum of love. In the vernacular of the prison he was a "rat." In his life were gathered up and expressed just about all the weaknesses possible to the human personality. But he was my patient, and therefore my opportunity to practise the ministry of healing. His worst weakness, a combination of insufferable self-pity and stubbornness, formed an almost insurmountable obstacle to any kind of medical treatment. He refused to cooperate in any way, and the prison doctor, thoroughly disgusted, was determined to send him into an isolation cell where he could stew in his own self-sustained misery. This to me, of course, was an admission of failure. I said so to the doctor and asked for time, hoping that some guidance as to an effective approach would come.

By and by this guidance emerged clear-cut in my consciousness. I had the "green light," and I knew exactly how I was to deal with this patient's character and experience.

I confided my conviction to the doctor and enlisted his cooperation. The work was done by a whispered conversation held by the doctor and me just as we had come out of the patient's room. We were outside his door, and partly concealed from him, but not beyond his range of hearing. I said to the doctor:

181

"This guy is the worst pest we've ever had in here. Every convict in the hospital hates him, and the sooner he kicks off the better. They all say it will be good riddance."

"Well, you'll not have long to wait," said the doctor. "A couple of weeks will finish up his little stretch. We can order a box for him now."

With this we walked away.

Thereupon the patient, driven by the relentless motive to defeat the hopes of his enemies, steeled his will against death, and began to take advantage of everything the hospital offered as an aid to his recovery. He got well.

The danger in this treatment lay in the possible inaccurate analysis of the patient's character. The same powerful suggestions given to a different type of man, could have as easily proved fatal. It was a case where the guidance had to be unmistakable. It was a case, also, which demonstrated the power of medicine and psychology when the two branches combine to produce a healing.

Spiritual. The wife of a high prison official was stricken while on a visit to her home, some three hundred miles from the prison. The emergency operation revealed peritonitis, that nightmare of every practising surgeon. The husband's telegram was placed in my hands. It revealed his terrible anxiety.

My first thought was: "If I only had a fraction of this anxiety, I should have the energy necessary to reach God." The idea behind the thought was that we must give in order to receive, and the more we have to give the greater is our capacity for receiving. The official and husband of the stricken woman had much to give in energy of fear and anxiety in return for perfect trust and peace. But he found himself too close to the one he loved, too attached to her, to be able to give her along with his own feelings away to God. Hence, I yearned for just a portion of his anxious care.

Since I didn't have this concern for the stricken woman, but was more or less indifferent in my feelings, I set about to evoke a genuine feeling of anxiety within myself as a preliminary to the following treatment.

In this connection I had only to think of the many things she had done and had tried to do in order to make prison life more endurable. As this list of her benefactions grew on the film of my memory, and as I contemplated the full meaning of her loss to all prisoners, I, too, began to feel deeply anxious about her. Within me there evolved a strong personal concern for her recovery. In meditation this feeling was steadily yielded up. At the point where I felt a saturation of peace and assurance in my consciousness, my meditation was over, and I went about my duties with no more concern in the matter. It was like an issue inevitably closed.

I have no way of knowing whether my meditation contributed anything to the woman's recovery. I can only believe that it did.

Combined methods. Out of solitary one day a prisoner was carried into the hospital in convulsions. Examination revealed a case of locked bowels. By the time the surgeon arrived the man was in a weak and dying condition. The surgeon declined to operate, saying that it would be nothing short of murder, since there was not even one chance in a million for the man to survive the operation.

I mentioned the fact that at the point where man was most hopeless, God was the most powerful. There was always a chance for His intercession. The surgeon was persuaded to take that chance.

The only preparation I could give the patient was suggestive therapy. He was told to go under the anaesthetic with his mind stayed on God. The major operation was successfully performed and the patient made a most gratifying recovery. Of his experience he told me the following story, however illusory it might be. He said that his other self, as he put it, went out of his body and remained above the operating table listening to everything that was said and seeing everything that was done. Many of these details he later recounted with interesting and rather amazing accuracy. However, his story was not taken seriously by either the resident physician or surgeon, and afterwards the man showed such an inclination to talk about his operation and especially of its supernatural aspects that he became a sort of laughing stock about the prison yard. Only a comparatively few were inclined to place any credence in this other self of his which hovered over his own well-carved body.

My hospital experience furnished me with an opportunity to practise and prove the things taught me by the old lifer. He gave me the principles. The hospital gave me latitude and choice for application. In the hospital his precept became example. As it turned out every spiritual healing observed was like the reading of an allegory. The process of effecting such healings was a parable in action. The patient got the healing, the healer got the parable. It was here that I learned that the healer knows best who is healed, just as certainly as the spiritual teacher knows best who is taught.

CHAPTER 18

THE VALUE OF TRAINING

THE YEARS FOLLOWING MY DUNGEON EXPERIENCE WERE cluttered with one kind of training or another. Much of this training was haphazard. Plans and programmes were started and abandoned. I was impatient often for immediate results. In consequence, adjustments to the new trend in my life were retarded. There was a lot of trial and error activity. And just as in the case of a novice starting out in crime the teachers and counsellors were many.

In prison where time hangs heavy on the souls of men, it is natural for those who are inclined toward religion to turn to the Bible for relief. Because of this you will find among prisoners a large number of very proficient Bible students. To these it is a delight when a new religious recruit is found emerging from the soggy marshlands of criminal philosophy. They are ever ready to extend a hand to the newcomer, to give counsel and teaching, and to point out ways for training in the spiritual life. The beginner's problem is not the availability of too little but of too much. Given more than he is able to assimilate, he attempts too great a variety of plans, with the result that he is frequently bogged down in despair.

The urgent need of the religious system in prisons is the making of more beginners, for once a man in prison shows signs of spiritual interest he immediately draws to him a new group of fellows who are able and eager, each in his own way, to give advice, sympathy, and understanding. This Christian missionary spirit in prison is one of society's best weapons in the ceaseless war against crime, if society only knew it. The prison chaplain has hundreds of

185

unknown aids in any large prison. His business it is to devise ways for wooing the new and ready recruits into the fold. There will be many to take hold of them once they have made the step in the Christ direction.

At the beginning of my criminal career I drew to me those who could help to shape my criminal character, or I was drawn to them. At the beginning of my spiritual career the same thing happened. I was not wanting for new friends and supporters, and sooner or later we found each other.

In this way I came to know many prisoners who were wonderfully read in the word of God as well as in other branches of literature, history, philosophy, science, biography, psychology. My contacts with them enriched my mind. Their fellowship was ennobling and stimulating.

The lifer was one of these. Of all my new-found friends and fellow prisoners he perhaps had the most lasting influence on my budding spiritual life. Partly this was due, no doubt, to my utter faith in him as a sincere friend, and my admiration for his learning and character. While he did much to guide, and instruct me in spiritual matters, he knew that eventually I should have to work out my own personal methods, and he told me so.

It seems to be an axiom of the inner life that, by and by, the aspirant must face the desires of the soul alone, and work out his approaches along lines indicated by individual need and capacity. In the last analysis, the method which fits the need of one unfolding soul will not fit the need of another. As below so above. As one man's food is another man's poison, so is the spiritual method of one a handicap to another. The teacher can take his pupil only so far. Then the pupil must press on alone. The Master finally withdraws from His disciples and leaves them to work out their own methods and ministries. From the need of mutual fellowship, however, we never escape, and all who live and work in a similar orbit draw inspiration, ideas, and encouragement one from another.

In my own development I found it efficacious to work out and follow a series of parallel methods of training. The following one I called "My seven-day plan." It gave me something different for each day in the week. To this end I brought to my mind seven single word concepts of God, which I listed in the following order: LOVE, LIGHT, LIFE, LAW, POWER, PEACE, JOY. Around each of the concepts I grouped all the scriptural references I could find as authority, support, and inspiration. As I worked methodically at this plan I discovered a general improvement in all the departments of my life and in the affairs I had with those around me.

FOR SUNDAY: THE TENDERNESS OF GOD

God is Love

Beloved, let us love one another: for love is of God; and every
one that loveth is born of God and knoweth God. He that
loveth not knoweth not God; for God is love.
—1 John 4:7-8.

Sunday, therefore, was reserved especially for the study and imitation of love, somewhat after the manner of Paul's injunction to the Ephesians, "Be ye therefore imitators of God, as beloved children and walk in love."

If the day caught me on an ebb tide of the spirit and I could not feel love I would imitate it by performing charitable services among my patients, which were not in the line of my duty. I would go out of my way to help them, and I would think of them in terms of lovingkindness, steadily refusing to see and amplify their faults.

At intervals throughout the day and night I would refresh myself with different love passages in the Bible, especially those found in the first epistle of John and in chapter 4. With the following passage I would sit down often: "God is love, and he that dwelleth in love, dwelleth in God, and God in him."

This would remind me that if God is love and is everywhere

present I literally lived and breathed and moved in a sea of love. Love was under me and over me and all around me and inside of me. My very cells floated in the solution of love. Closing my eyes I would give myself up to this reflection and try to realize it in my deep inner consciousness. Often in this way I would recapture the feeling as I had known it in the dungeon, and then I could apprehend with Paul: "That Christ may dwell in your hearts by faith; that ye, being rooted and grounded in love, may be able to comprehend with all saints what is the breadth, and length, and depth, and height."

Having established this comprehension and glow, I would then set out upon a visiting round of my patients. Always it seemed to be given to me to place the right touch here, say the right word there, and do a favour in the right place at the right time. I learned the need, also, of taking time out for this sort of preparation before going into the operating room or entering upon any important piece of work.

At the close of one of our meetings a girl came up and asked for an interview. She tended the switchboard in the stock exchange. She had been there a year and every day of it had been agony and apprehension. She had a girl co-worker next to her who had formed a jealous dislike for her, and who did everything she could to make her fearful for her job. At this time the girl was on the verge of a nervous breakdown.

She was advised to prepare herself spiritually each morning before going to work; to do her best to evoke the love-consciousness for her job and all with whom she came in contact, and especially for her co-worker.

Her problem was fear, fear of this other girl's opinions and threats. She was told to memorize 1 John 4:18: "There is no fear in love; but perfect love casteth out fear; because fear hath torment. He that feareth is not made perfect in love."

"Fill your mind with loving thoughts," we told her, "for this girl, control your reactions to her jealousy, overcome her with good, melt her with love, and she will turn out to be the very means which will lead you on to higher and better things."

It was not an easy accomplishment, for it is never easy to shift from a fear-state to a love-state. The girl struggled and we encouraged her along with letters. After a few weeks she caught the rhythm of it and was able to establish and maintain the loving mood. Her enemy melted and became a friend. They both rose steadily to higher positions. The girl is now a private secretary to a man of large affairs.

One Sunday afternoon, after I had been practising the love method all day, a young man was removed from his cell to the hospital. He was physically depleted and was in a dangerous state of mind and emotions. He was doubled up with acute indigestion. The doctor was not present. Due to his rundown condition generally it was an emergency case, and the doctor in charge, a prisoner, was plainly alarmed for his life.

I sat down on the edge of his bed and took his hand. My mood immediately had a salutary effect upon him. By and by I could inquire into his prison experience. I soon discovered that he was a victim to fear and the first offender's deadliest enemy, grief. He was painfully religious underneath his mask, intensely sensitive to sin. He feared God's judgment of him, and he grieved over the disgrace his crime had brought upon his mother and sister.

I talked to him about the tenderness of God, and pointed out that His mercy far exceeded His judgments. I quoted the passage that has done so much for so many who, as this youth, had come under the devastating force of the sin-complex: "Herein is love, not that we loved God, but that He loved us, and sent His Son to be the propitiation for our sins." "Listen, kid," he was told, "you don't belong to sin. You belong to Christ. In him your sins are forgiven. Now just put your hand in his, and everything will be all right."

He relaxed as I sat holding his hand. He fell into a deep restful sleep. He slept through the afternoon and night, and woke the next morning refreshed and healed.

Love is the most dynamic power in the universe. It is the universal medium by virtue of which the creative principle in life operates.

When we are in the love-consciousness the principle of creation works through us. Every moment we love something is created in and through us. Put love to the most humble task and it becomes exalted and takes on hues of creative importance. Food prepared in love, when eaten, moves harmoniously through the system, fully nourishing the body. Home cooking has its indisputable place of honour, not because it is cooked better, but because, generally speaking, home-cooking spells love-cooking. A meal cooked hastily by a cook whose only interest is quitting time and wages requires a cast-iron stomach to digest it. It is poisonous to a normal person. That is why prison food, regardless of its quality, is so often at the bottom of prison discontent. It is the cause of the common disease of constipation so prevalent in our prisons. The best *chefs,* the most sought after, and the highest priced are those who love their profession.

No home can fail, except at the point where love goes out. Bring love back and the home comes back. Poverty cannot exist where love is. A business founded on love and maintained in love cannot avoid prospering within and without, materially as well as spiritually. A church that stands for goodness and mercy, for love as well as righteousness will be unable to hold the crowds, for just as the multitudes pressed in upon Jesus, the embodiment of the Great Love, so will the multitude press in on the church that embodies and radiates love. People are drawn as by a magnet to the dwelling place of love.

Love is the source of inspiration and revelation. It is the source of both mundane and spiritual genius, and it is the perfume, the substance, and fullness of God. If a man is feeble in love, he is impotent in life, for love is the abundance of life. If a man achieve the whole world and be lacking in love his life is but a shallow mockery, a miserable sham, a pitiful husk, empty and frail, and ugly, and he becomes a slithering piper of hollow sounds, shunned by animals, repulsive to children, avoided by humanity, a sounding brass and a tinkling cymbal.

The Value of Training

Professional nurses should be trained in the spiritual science of love, for a love-filled nurse can do more for the sick than a dozen doctors who are lacking in love. The secret of the old family doctor's success was love, for he had little in the way of medicine and equipment. The world's lasting personalities are those who showed love and mercy. The haters, the destroyers, the greed-enslaved tycoons pale on the pages of history, while the great lovers, with Jesus at their head, grow brighter with the passing of time. No one is worth remembering for anything except the love he expressed during life. And love should be allowed to overflow. To be afraid to love is cowardly. To withhold love where it is needed is traitorous. To degrade love is blasphemous. To think of love as something weak and pollyannish, sensual and destructive, is to be self-indicted of ignorance, and to be self-divorced from life's greatest power and sweetest joy.

On these Sundays I had set aside for the exclusive practice of the love method there was always a Sabbath quiet and harmony in the hospital. There seemed to be less departmental friction, and a more noticeable expression of friendliness among the members of the hospital staff. The patients, too, displayed less irritation, and seemed more willing to conform to medical routine. They fretted less under the limitations imposed upon them by hospital rules. These results were not only noticeable to me, but were often commented upon by others in the hospital, especially by the outside visitors who, in some cases, were permitted admittance on this day.

It was a frequent and pleasurable experience on Sunday to have a patient, with no persuasion, voluntarily indicate that he desired to discuss something along spiritual lines.

On one such occasion an assiduous student of the world's great agnostics, a man who at the time was a bed patient, surprised me. I had asked him if I could read something for him. He said, "I'd like it, very much."

"What magazine would you like?" I asked.

"I wish," he replied, "that you'd read the whole 27th chapter of Acts." I did so. "Would you care to discuss it?" he asked.

I spent one of the most interesting and profitable hours of that day discussing the foreknowledge, which was one of the illumined Paul's many gifts.

"I've neither accepted nor rejected God," the patient said. "But of all those who have declared His reality, Paul has been the one who has most nearly persuaded me."

He had handed me the golden key to his heart. It was a delicate and precious key. Well did I know that. It had to be used entirely under divine guidance. With it in my hand I had to be absolutely certain of my spiritual intuition. The slightest misuse or false turn of that key and all would have been lost. When he was discharged from the hospital the Apostle Paul had persuaded and convinced him. He had come in a brilliant agnostic. He left an humble and wistful yearner after the Master of men.

I look back upon those prison Sundays from a vantage point of good health, good will, and expansive living. To them I owe much.

FOR MONDAY: THE GUIDANCE OF GOD

God is Light

Even so let your light shine before men, that they
may see your good works, and glorify your Father
which is in Heaven. —Matthew 5:16.

Monday was reserved for *works* and *beingness*, wooing the guidance of God, walking in the light of God, and performing the will of God in works. It was a day in which the thoughts and feelings and willings and workings were tested beforehand by the self-enquiry, "Does this glorify the Father?"

On Monday people return to the business of work, after the Sabbath lull. "Blue Monday," this day is called. To think of it as such is to begin the work week under a heavy handicap, for the way of beginning a day, a week, a month, or a year may well determine the outcome of the day, the week, the month, the year. Not necessarily! But why begin wrong? Why take a chance? Why impose any limitation at all? There is light in the statement, "To know how to begin is to know how to finish."

Monday, having a dark reputation, became the correct day for practising the presence of light. It is the badge of great workmanship to have succeeded where once one has failed. At the darkest place is the place to hold up the light. Christ's disciples failed him most at Jerusalem. Here he had them tarry; here to begin their ministry; at this place of their failure they achieved undying success. What they did here will light the pathway of men until the last weary and timeworn straggler has found his way into the eternal fold. *It pays huge dividends to do the hard thing under spiritual direction. To every woman comes a difficult day. Being the most difficult it holds forth to her a golden opportunity. If she can live the spiritual life now, if she can let her light shine now, do the will of God, and perform works unto His glory, great shall be her success.*

It is promised of God, and He will not fail: "And when I passed by thee, and saw thee polluted in thine own blood, I said unto thee when thou wast in thy blood, LIVE; yea, I said unto thee when thou wast in thy blood, LIVE." —Ezekiel 16:8. It is a double witness, and the double witness from the spiritual world always means certainty. Hence this promise is certain. *The more difficult the task or the problem the more spiritual power is released, when the thing is seized upon as an opportunity to glorify God.*

On Mondays I would devote much time seeking the guidance of God. There are many kinds of spiritual guidance. There is the guidance that warns, or releases an alarm within. It is the lesser guidance. There is the common hunch, which is the least. These are apt to make more use of the red and yellow light, danger and caution, than they are of the green light to proceed. They are more likely to say "No." Inhibition rather than exhibition chiefly characterizes the least and lesser guidance. Intuition, the highest of directive guidance, always says, "Yes." It is ever the green light, and knows nothing of alarm, warning, negation. It is the positive voice within, but is *still* and *small*. It whispers but once, and is gone with the slightest inattention. The more purely spiritual a thing becomes the more jealous it is of us, the more it demands our undivided attention.

Spiritual intuition is developed, like brain and muscle, by exercise. When stillness is cultivated and the art of inner listening has been perfected, the *still small voice* speaks often. It grows when given instant attention, and when its directions are acted upon promptly. It never says, "Don't." It always says, "Do."

Finally there is the Great Guidance, which is the work of the Holy Spirit who guides us into all truth. The Holy Spirit is as inevitably one with His Word as the air is one with earth. The air cannot be separated from the earth it envelops. If this happened both would cease to exist as life-producing and life-sustaining instruments in the solar scheme. Nor can the Holy Spirit be separated from His Word. It is through His Word that the Holy Spirit reveals truth to us, guidance and protection, revelation, light. It is, therefore, the mark of good judgment to keep the mind well stocked with scriptural passages. For it is through these that the Holy Spirit will bring the great truths to our remembrance.

Hence on Mondays, I lived much with the Bible, reading it, and committing occasional passages to memory.

When the Holy Spirit speaks to another through us, it will come as a flash out of our memory, an apt piece of scripture to fill the need just at the right time, in the right place. The best practising psychologists and counsellors are those with a religious background, whose minds have been supplied with the Word of God.

I shall point out three examples of this. When this High Guidance is genuine the quoted scripture is never a preachment. It is re-creative life. Nor is it rejected, because its release is perfectly timed. It falls only into a receptive state of consciousness. It does not come through by pre-arrangement; but is wholly spontaneous. The counsellor places himself between the need and the supply, he himself being empty but willing to be used. The need is the person to be helped. The Holy Spirit is the supply. The counsellor is the intermediary. The supply is given through the Word of God, which is as a seed dropped into prepared soil at the right time and in the right way. Out of this seed bursts new life for the needful one, a new light breaks and re-creation takes place.

Bad Tom was a Negro serving ninety-nine years for murder. He was recognized as a dangerous man by his fellow convicts and a bad actor by the prison officials. Bad Tom was a successful agitator. His speciality was to foment trouble between the black and white sections of the prison population. Many bloody battles had been traced to his agitations. There was a clever streak in him. He could always start the trouble, and somehow manage to keep out of the actual battle himself, and thus avoid solitary confinement for fighting.

It was because of this cleverness that he landed in the hospital with a serious stab wound between his shoulder blades. He was knifed by a man of his own race on the day this man got out of solitary where he had paid the price for a fight which Bad Tom had instigated and had avoided himself.

The wounded Negro thought he was going to die. Because of his reputation, the white men who attended him in the hospital did nothing to discourage this fatal notion. If anything, it was indirectly encouraged. Bad Tom found himself dangerously wounded in a hospital manned mostly by white men whom he was known to hate. It was not a pleasant position for him. He was in the enemy's camp, helplessly in the hands of those against whom he had declared eternal war.

The situation was most favourable for me who was practising the presence of God through men in extremity. Out of the white ranks of his avowed enemies, one would step forward with an outstretched hand. I decided that Bad Tom was my opportunity. At whatever price to my own popularity I decided that he needed a friend more than he had ever needed one in his life. I would be that friend.

In this demonstration of friendship I gained an influence over Bad Tom that was close to supernatural. All the normal barriers went down and I was permitted to probe into every crack and niche of his natural, psychological, and spiritual life. I administered to his needs with love and medical attention. I went beyond his needs and supplied many of his wants. I guided our talks into spiritual channels. I confided to him. I inspired him with vivid examples of the spiritual life. I fanned the feeble spark in his soul until it burst into flame. I made him hunger and thirst after the soul's life. When I felt that he was ready, I went to my room, read the Sermon on the Mount, and then offered myself up in silent submission to guidance.

Immediately afterwards I went to Bad Tom's bedside, drew up a chair, and asked what he had on his mind.

"I wish I could know God," he said.

He had thrown the door wide open and exposed the need. I had not the slightest idea what he was going to say, or what I was going to say in reply. The answer came through my being and out over my lips, "Blessed are the peacemakers: for they shall be called the children of God." A moment of silence followed this. Without further speech I rose and went out. I knew the work was done, because I had not done it. It was done by One who knows what He is about. I left that room with a sense of the utmost certainty.

Bad Tom got well and became a prison peacemaker, just the reverse of what he had been. When God does the job He does it well. It was so in Tom's case. The qualifying word, bad, vanished from his name. His very presence in a group of prisoners seemed to establish a condition of peacefulness and ward off arguments.

Johnny was a baseball pitcher, the most popular man on the prison's first team. He was a true athlete who lived a clean, moral life. In trying to protect a friend he had committed perjury and was sentenced. The blood of fair play and good sportsmanship ran in his veins.

One of his curving speed balls struck a batter in the head. The man never did entirely recover. He suffered lapses of memory, and frightful headaches. Not long after he was released he died.

Johnny began to pine away under a sense of guilt and condemnation. Everyone tried to comfort and divert him. His friends reasoned with him that the accident had been unavoidable, that it had not been his fault. But Johnny continued to brood and go down physically. Finally he was committed indefinitely to the hospital.

In cultivating Johnny's friendship and confidence I was guided to avoid all mention of his tragedy, and to employ the utmost tact and diplomacy in my efforts to manoeuvre his thinking into spiritual channels. To accomplish this it took much time and prayer and love.

The rewards came slowly at first. I discovered that the only subject that would divert his attention for any length of time was Papini's description of the Crucifixion scene. So we talked much about this. One day I was able to hold his attention for an hour, exclusively on this subject. The conversation was closed with these words, which came through me, "Forgive them, Father, for they know not what they do."

This became the seed that found deep soil in the consciousness of Johnny. It grew steadily as he pondered it. He had not struck the player intentionally, and he became convinced of the fact that he had been absolved from all blame. His sense of guilt faded away and he was again free, though he pitched no more baseball.

Jerry was a young man in his early twenties. He had been twice in Reform School, and was now serving his first indeterminate sentence in the penitentiary. He landed in a hospital bed with a nervous breakdown, a victim of exaggerated self-abuse.

Convicts, like children, can be exceedingly cruel to each other, and like certain types of religionists, they can be insufferably smug, fatuous, and self-righteous. Because Jerry had sunk deeper into the sewer of sexual degeneracy than anyone else in prison, the hospital attendants drew their righteous skirts and affected nausea in the boy's presence. There was a silent but concerted intention to ostracize Jerry and studiously to avoid him. Again this influence of the devil played into my hands, for I just as studiously decided to seek and cultivate him. Jerry became my friend.

I got the fragments out of him a little at a time and pieced his story together. It took some such shape as this: His mother had been endowed with two talents, one for writing and one for painting. Lacking the energy and the drive to perfect these talents, she married instead and gave herself over to the job of raising a large family. Jerry had been her firstborn, and the talents for writing and drawing soon began to show themselves in his life.

However, his father, hard-pressed to earn a living, was indifferent; his mother, equally hard-pressed, did not encourage her son. Around the age of puberty these unsatisfied creative energies in Jerry began to express themselves through antisocial habits of conduct and behaviour. The end was Reform School and ultimately prison.

Both in Reform School and prison Jerry was a problem for the officials. His chief offence was the writing and circulating of obscene stories and the drawing and circulating of obscene pictures.

Though his stories were the result of a diseased imagination, they nevertheless were fashioned with skill, and plainly showed that he possessed a sure intuitive knowledge of literary effects and all the properties that go into the making of a closely-knit and correctly developed short story.

There was nothing wrong with Jerry's convict literature except his subject matter. I began to approach his better nature along the line of his predominant talent and interest.

I told him there had been written one perfect short story, one matchless essay, and one unequalled discourse. At his request I named these masterpieces: "The Prodigal Son," "The 13th Chapter of 1st Corinthians," and "The Sermon on the Mount."

Making these dogmatic statements was like making a master key. Having made them I had to prove them. This led to a discussion and analysis of each one. I saw to it that this discussion and analysis went on and on. I stated over and over that Paul's essay on love was a matchless piece of work. This insistence became a challenge to Jerry. I got paper and pencil for him and he set about to match the Apostle's great work. These attempts he would pass to me, and I would point out, by comparison, where they failed to equal the model.

The details of Jerry's labours, the sweat and blood and tears, may be passed up. In the end this writing programme had so completely reconditioned his consciousness that it was impossible for him to sink again from the lofty to the degraded themes.

Jerry was healed thoroughly in his moral parts. He embraced Christ. He literally lived with the letters of Paul. For the rest of his sentence his spare time was devoted to writing religious hymns, poems, essays, editorials, and stories.

My guidance in this case had victory in it from the outset, because it was founded in the Word of God.

In the world to-day there is a tendency to depend more and more on divine guidance, and to seek help from others less and less. This is a splendid tendency, which will pay the seeker well, for, "If any man lack wisdom, let him ask of God, and it shall be given him." Especially is it good to ask at night, the last thing before falling asleep, for, "He giveth unto His beloved in sleep."

By making Monday a day for practising the presence of light, and a day for searching diligently in the scriptures for references which showed God as Light, the universal blueness and lassitude of that much maligned day vanished from my existence.

I can say out of this personal experience in training that my faith in divine guidance was greatly reinforced, and that through this training there did come a steady expansion of my perceptive, conceptive, and reflective faculties. The faculty of spiritual intuition was increasingly set free, and in general, the training had a decided influence for good in my life, leading to improvement in all the areas of my personality, within and without.

However, I would remind the reader that I am reporting my own experience, and can only guess what the same method of training may achieve in the life of another.

FOR TUESDAY: THE ABUNDANCE OF GOD

God is Life

The thief cometh not, but for to steal, and to kill, and to destroy: I am come that they might have life, and that they might have it more abundantly. —John 10:10.

This was the great passage for me, a lifelong thief, for by the most vivid experience I knew how terribly true it was. I had lived to destroy, and had been destroyed. Joy is life. I had known no joy. Creative work is life. I had done only destructive work and involuntary prison labour under bitter protest and nerve-tearing rebellion. Play is life. I had sacrificed the spirit of play.

The things of life are born. The things of death are imposed. Limitless life *is*. Limitation is invented. The thing upon which life plays and through which life acts is made. The things which correspond to life are born. My body had been made. In it life had been born. My physical birth had been but the delivery of a fashioned form. The life in it had been born. The form would change. The life would remain. The form, while it endured, could experience the abundance of life or the limitation of life, according as I, the occupant, chose.

I could belong to the limited life and be in bondage, or the limitless life could belong to me and set me free.

And so I put aside Tuesday as the day for studying and practising the unlimited, the abundant life. And in this practice and study I reached for Him who could and would give me the life I sought. And He said to me, "I am the good shepherd: the good shepherd giveth his life for the sheep."

I would go to the chapel and observe the morning visitors. They were Christians, and I would marvel that they reflected so little of life in their bodies and personalities. They so often seemed spiritless, heavy, and over-serious, as though they knew nothing of vibrant health and joy, as though they had lost the power to smile. I marvelled that our chaplain showed so little of the radiant contagion of life.

"Surely," I thought, "these people want the abundant life in all the areas of their personalities. Why do they refuse to accept?" I would enquire concerning this curious question, and I would be told that Christians did not all believe in asking for the abundant life on earth; that they wanted it enough, but felt they should not ask God for gifts that would bring joy. And then I would wonder if I had read my Bible amiss, if I had failed to understand the Giver of Life: "Therefore I say unto you, what things soever ye desire, believe that ye receive them, and ye shall have them." Could this be a mistranslation, or if spoken by the Master, was he dealing in levity?

My Gospels showed me Jesus proclaiming over and over the message of life on earth, here and now, pleading almost, "Whosoever will, let him take the water of life freely."

And Christian visitors would come into the hospital. I could understand why the convict patients were ill and expressed so little of the vibrant quality of life. I was confused by the Christian visitors. They seemed to move in a dark circle of tenseness and strain. The twinkle of interest and spontaneity was missing in their eyes. The vocabulary they used was weighted down with negative observations and conclusions. Among prisoners they exuded an atmosphere of fear, doubt, superiority, judgment. They made me want to approach them out of sympathy. Yet they put up a reserve that repulsed me. I could only stand off and weep inside.

And during these years in the outside world I have gone about among Christians, and I have seen them impose, consciously and deliberately, the same limitations upon life as criminals impose ignorantly upon life. I have seen them yield to perpetual hate and pay and pay for their treason upon life. I have heard them gossip about personalities and shrivel as the stream of life went dry. I have seen them shifting the blame, nursing the resentment, mothering the grudge. I have seen them in their mental cups intoxicated with worry, anxiety, the fear of life and the fear of death—makers of thoughts and feelings that cut the jugular veins of the rich full life. And I've wondered, confused, befuddled, amazed.

During the many years I myself had lived after this fashion I had lived a living death. By hating I refused to give access to the abundant life. And by constantly imposing limitations upon life I alienated myself from life-gladness, I divorced myself from the health of mind, emotions, body, soul.

For Tuesday, therefore, life was my theme and practice. The abundant life of God!

I found in my scripture that which constituted the constricted life and the expanded life. I found the bridge from the former to the latter. I found the simple rules of the road. In the Epistle of James I got the green light: "Is any among you afflicted? Let him pray." Here was the answer to those who had imposed limitations upon the flow of life. "Is any merry? Let him sing psalms." Here was the reward for those who had loosed the floodgates of life.

My course of practice in the prison hospital was clear and unmistakable. I was not to go around in search of darkness. I was not to walk in gloom, suspicion, irritation, amplifying my own and others' faults and conditions. I was to walk lightly with a merry heart, a cheerful voice, a contagious smile, with a song in my heart and a psalm in my soul. Hence Tuesday was a great day for me. Every conquest over my negative self came as a thrill. Every spontaneous up-bubbling of joyfulness filled me with gratitude.

And here were my patients—opportunities for the practice of life. Upon this special day, what would be my attitude toward them? What would be my rule of action? Intercessory prayer! The exercise of faith! For, "And the prayer of faith shall save the sick, and the Lord shall raise him up; and if he have committed sins, they shall be forgiven him." Even the *respectable sins,* which were the most pernicious because self-condoned, would be forgiven: *the sins of worry, envy, selfishness, avarice, gossip, resentment, fault-finding, intolerance, self-satisfaction, pride—all these destroyers of life would be forgiven.*

The sins of the imagination, which wallowed in lust secretly, and pursued life-retarding infamies beneath the surface—these, too, would be forgiven, and the reward of life would come to their victims through the prayer of faith.

On this day, if Christian visitors came, I would not look for their faults, their limitations, their failure to express life. I would keep a prayer in my heart for their victory, a song of gratitude for their possibilities. And then they would reflect these things to me.

The prayer for my patients would first be for myself. To see them as Jesus would see them! Then both patient and nurse would profit.

It is a difficult rule to follow, and my score was not always large. The practice proved, however, that *it pays to look beyond the appearance to the possibility.* It is the easiest thing in the world to find fault with a Christian, a spiritual teacher, a religious counsellor, and to see in him one's own faults, as in a mirror held up, for finally one's neighbour boils down to oneself. The possibilities of Christianity are the world's hopes. The critical observations of Christianity are the world's despairs, when these observations deal with surface appearances, and they are most devastating when they come from Christians themselves.

In the hospital was a patient in whom the sands of life were running low. About a year prior to this time an educational drive had been let loose in the Press against the increase of cancer victims. All the symptoms of the dread disease were exposed by medical authorities. This man had followed the campaign with the avidity of a movie fan. Being susceptible to negative suggestion, some of these symptoms turned up in his own body and he concluded that he, too, was a cancer victim.

Constipation and indigestion, common ills among prisoners, began to assume an alarming importance to him. He dwelt negatively upon them until they became a genuine menace. He underwent a severe cauterizing operation for stomach ulcers. He was certain the operation had not healed him. He brooded on this conviction. Three months later examination revealed that he was a victim of stomach cancer.

Here was limitation imposed upon life in a large way, and though his condition had been hysterically produced, it was nevertheless as life-depleting as though it had been organically legitimate. The patient's life was slowly ebbing away.

I began to employ both intercessory and conversational prayer in his case, and while in his presence, to practise the policy of joyfulness, keeping out of my own consciousness the morbid observations and negative conclusions.

My intercessory prayers for him were offered up in the privacy of my own room. My conversational prayers were given as I sat on the edge of his bed, ministering to his needs, or while holding his hand. It was here that I learned about the efficacy of conversational prayer.

There are three requirements for this type of prayer to make it dynamic and re-creative: *first*, the conversation must be organized around a spiritual subject; *second,* those conversing must have a mutual interest in the subject; *third,* argument, controversy, and negative discussion of personalities should be eliminated, or reduced to a minimum.

Three results are obtained in conversational prayer: *first,* revelation through the spontaneous exchange of spiritual ideas; *second,* the elimination of weariness and fatigue, the irritating or heavy sense of Time and the monotony of Place; *third,* a steady expansion of life and the frontier of fellowship and joy.

When two persons can meet these requirements, an hour's discussion, exclusively devoted to a spiritual subject, leaves them refreshed in every way. Their faith is enriched, their souls are released, their tensions are gone. They are vital, alert, magnetic, charged with love and goodwill, and are vibrant with physical energy and aliveness. Until the clutch of negative life has once more taken hold of them and claimed them, they irradiate an expansive and contagious spirit of life.

In connection with this particular patient it was necessary first to stimulate his interest in some spiritual subject, and then prompt him to express his views on it. In this way he could be induced to lose himself for the time in a subject that was greater than himself and in an expression of life that swallowed up the limited life of the sick mind and sick body. I noticed that these spiritual conversations always had a tonic effect upon him, which would last until he had again lapsed into his habitual mode of morbid thinking. However, as the conversations continued, the spiritual afterglow became more lasting.

In this way he was in time re-educated in his thinking processes, and of course, with this accomplishment his self-created and self-imposed disease vanished, and he possessed the more abundant life.

Now this man of his own free will never would have responded to the injunction of James to pray. I might have told him that prayer had the solution to his problem, which would have been true. But knowing him as I did, I knew such an approach would have been repelled, with the result that my perfectly good intentions would have done more harm than good.

When the mountain will not come, however, one goes to the mountain. When there is opposition to one kind of prayer it is removed by introducing another kind. To this day my patient, if he is alive, does not know that he gained his healing by means of prayer.

Into the world we come with the gift of life, God's life, and God's life is never constricting but is always expansive. Where His life *is*, unfailing growth *is* in us. In His life "we live and move and have our being." In His life we climb "from glory to glory." In His life we grow, "First the blade, then the ear, then the full corn in the ear." His life is the uplifter and expander of our life; it is creator and re-creator of our life. Out of His life our life originates and procreates. In His limitless life our limited life evolves. In His abundant life our stunted life is fed. In His perfect life our afflicted life is healed. In His eternal life our mortal life puts on the garments of immortality.

God's life never changes; but it changes our life. God's life is fullness, and if we want the fullness of life we must appropriate it by letting it use us. We must give ourselves to it. Nor can one single negative thought or negative feeling appropriate one single inch of expansion into God's life, except by His infinite mercy and grace.

To fear His judgments is to throw ourselves upon His charity. We are objects of Divine Charity when we doubt His love and mercy by our expressions of fear, when we prolong the sense of guilt and morbidly enjoy the abnormal emotions, when we linger in the valley of self-condemnation and sin-consciousness, when we deceive ourselves into thinking that our blue mood delights God and our radiant joy and rejoicing spirits offend Him. All negative thinking, from a spiritual point of view, is destructive thinking, and all negative thinkers are objects of God's charity.

The Value of Training

The thing that delights God is our appropriation of His life. We lay claim to this inheritance every time we think a holy, unselfish thought, every time we love unselfseekingly, every time we admit His life as our life, every time we express wholesome joy and spontaneous gladness. We put on more of God's abundant life every time we forgive another, every time we aid another correctly, every time we let anger out and poise in. We appropriate God's life when we pray and engage in spiritual meditation and silence, when we read and digest and assimilate His Immortal Word. We claim God's life when we give Him ours; when we empty ourselves of *self* His life flows in.

In these Tuesdays I discovered many, many things, and many, many ways for practising the life of God and for laying hold of my portion of its abundance.

Sometimes I am asked the following question "Wasn't the prison life very hard to endure after your experience?"

It makes no difference where your body is when you can live in the expansiveness of God's eternal life. You may be on land or on the sea, in the air or beneath the earth; you may be in a hovel or a mansion, in a dungeon cell or a living room; you may be a ruler or a peasant, an executive or a labourer—wherever you are or whatever you are, if God's life belongs to you and you are claiming it, yours is the happy onward-going towards the glorious sunrise, for in your life there can be no setting sun, no death, and no bondage to the natural processes of mortal decline. To you life must ever be a Divine Romance, a breathless drama, a colourful pageant, an endless procession and adventure, with ebb-tides and barren valleys, with sterile interludes interwoven as contrast against which the victories are made to glow all the brighter.

I look back upon those latter prison months with only gratitude and delight, never with regret and a sense of shame. Those Tuesday practices showed me the way into life as it ought to be—ever more abundant, ever more expanding, ever more exhilarating and useful.

FOR WEDNESDAY: THE PRINCIPLE OF GOD

God is Law

The law is truth. —Psalm 119:142.
The law of the Lord is perfect. —Psalm 19:7.

I made it a habit to start this day with a petition, "Open thou mine eyes that I may behold wondrous things out of thy law." And then I would reaffirm that every action has its cause in the law of Good, and that out of the fruits of every action could be found evidence of the law of Good, no matter how corrupt or bitter those fruits appeared to be. I would assure myself that there was no such thing as a bad person. There were those who, lacking in wisdom, and hence in a genuine self-interest, misapplied or misused the law of Good.

In this way I trained myself to look deeper into the fruits of action until I could perceive the good through the enveloping fog of evil. The more evil a man appeared to others the more certain I was of him as an opportunity for me to practise the finding of good. For my model and example I took Jesus who was prone to pick up those whom the world rejected. If a man or boy was being rejected and pushed down by my fellow co-workers, he became my chance. I would place myself between him and God, and with one hand in his and one hand in God's I would permit myself to be lifted up. My friend would then be drawn up with me. This was the manner of Jesus. He placed one hand in the hand of sin-ravished humanity, the other, in the hand of his Father, because "If I be lifted up I will draw all men to me."

I want to emphasize this particular phase of my Wednesday practice, because of its good effects on my life, and because it banishes even a hidden belief that the lifting power came from my own brain and nerves and sinews. The power was from God and was given by virtue of the law of God's good. The practice made me aware that "of myself I can do nothing."

The Value of Training

Wednesday was the day reserved for the practice of obedience. The supreme law of God was accepted as the Law of Love, or Good. My objective for this day, therefore, was to drill myself in this Supreme Law of Love by practising the *love of law*.

To this end I sought to be more obedient to the laws of the prison, even to those which had long been obsolete but had not been removed from the rule card. Many of these laws, or prison rules, had been made years before, and had been adapted to a prison system that no longer existed, for instance, the law of silence. The silence ban had been lifted twenty years before, but had not been freed of the "talk within reason" clause. Hence on this day I made an effort to keep within that clause. I would speak only when it was necessary in the line of duty. If a question was asked I gave the answer fully, but added no extra comments. Nor did I answer in such a way as to prompt another question or further discussion.

I committed no act knowingly that would have been a violation of state or Federal law had I been on the outside.

On this day I made a special effort to observe the laws of health, the laws of emotion, and the laws of mind. I sought to think positive, constructive thoughts and to evoke and prolong peaceful and other salutary feelings.

On this day I would write considerably, but slowly, having for my main object the practice of obedience to the laws of grammar and rhetoric, to the extent of my knowledge of them. The same care was observed in my speech. I made a special effort to obey the special laws governing the hospital nurses and attendants.

This practice brought to my mind a fuller appreciation of the diversity and multiplicity of natural and divine laws and proved an excellent drill in self-control and concentrated inquiry.

It made me aware, also, that while God was Principle He was something more. Love and Grace, for instance, and the Creator of principle. The practice revealed to me that I could not petition

Principle, since it was a mechanical law in the universe, which operated on the basis of unfailing precision, and could not go outside its own fixed place to answer my prayer. It would not hear my prayer. Nor could it violate itself to answer. Therefore God as Law was to be applied. Not petitioned. For a petition presupposed two things: the petitioner who prayed and the God who heard. Two personalities were involved: one finite with a need, and the other Infinite with the supply. This gave me a God with a personality composed of all the spiritual qualities, and it personalized and individualized Him for me in the being of Jesus Christ. In this manner the whole problem of Deity was removed from the realm of vague abstraction and gave me a feeling of intimacy with God who was full of mercy and grace and wisdom, just as Jesus presented Him in the Parable of the Prodigal Son, a close, warm Father of infinite love for a wilful and wayward child who had strayed far from His home and counsel and from His protection and understanding and from the abundance Jesus had symbolized in the robe and shoes and fatted calf. With such a Heavenly Father a Reality for me, I was able to sidestep most of the bewildering pitfalls that beset the path of the Greeks, the intellectual religionists, of whom Paul spoke, "The God whom you ignorantly worship Him declare I unto you."

Shortly before I left prison I was given a knowledge of my position in the plan of things. Without being aware of the plan I had successfully used it on my Wednesday practices of the Law of Good.

Man is a citizen of two worlds, the material and the spiritual. Standing between them he is impressed and influenced by both. These worlds separate themselves into kingdoms. Below man is the mineral kingdom, the vegetable kingdom, and the animal kingdom. These lower kingdoms are composed of conditions, and man corresponds to them in accordance with their conditioning laws. Nutrition, for example, is a law. It is also a condition imposed. If for any reason a man ceases to correspond to this condition he will die of starvation. If his correspondence is inadequate he will suffer from malnutrition. Oxygenation of the blood is a law, and it is a condition imposed upon man by nature. If man does not correspond to this law and condition he ceases to live. And so it goes throughout all the kingdoms of the material world.

The spiritual world also is made up of kingdoms. They are, immediately above man, the Divine Kingdom, the Angelic Kingdom, the Celestial Kingdom. These higher kingdoms are composed of states of consciousness.

Man swings like a sponge between these two worlds, attracting to him and absorbing the divine states from above and the material conditions from below. Briefly and more specifically the order of these kingdoms and man's position in them is as follows:

The Celestial Kingdom
The Angelic Kingdom
The Divine Kingdom

Human Kingdom

The Animal Kingdom
The Vegetable Kingdom
The Mineral Kingdom

The above kingdoms are also differing grades of heaven; i.e., of the spiritual consciousness. One may enter the Divine Kingdom and be able to report to the world what he saw and felt there. Beyond this experience he cannot report his findings to the world. In the experience of Paul he was "snatched up to the third heaven, and there saw things unspeakable"; i.e., having experienced Ultimate Reality, he could not report what he saw and felt to finite consciousness.

Now these higher kingdoms are governed by divine laws, the laws of spiritual states of consciousness. Obedience to these heavenly laws stands for the application of them in the human kingdom. On the other hand, when a man engages in prayer or worship or spiritual meditation he is employing the highest obedience and is making the most efficacious application of the spiritual laws and states.

Man is higher than the animal in evolution; but if, through ignoring the kingdoms above him, he yields to sensuality, avarice, self-ishness, he can and does sink below the level of the beasts, over which God has decreed that he shall take dominion. In fact, it is God's injunction that man shall take dominion over all the conditional world. The only way he can do this is by the spiritual power given to him from the kingdoms above. And this taking dominion over the material world boils down to overcoming his own human nature, for he embodies all that is below and possesses the potential capacity for all that is above. To take dominion over oneself, therefore, is to conquer the world. It is the heavenly power that can sublimate or spiritualize the world conditions. Hence the accurate advice of Jesus to man, "Seek first the kingdom of heaven and all these things will be added unto you."

As a result of engaging in spiritual activity the divine states are drawn down into material conditions to redeem them and bring them into harmony with themselves. Thus when one sends up praise to God, blessings (spiritual states) come down in strict accordance with the operation of the law of cause and effect, or the law of attraction which causes like to attract like.

The reader will see by this why I considered my patients as opportunities for practising the divine presence; why my attitude towards them was that they were serving me, giving me a chance to help myself. Whether or not my services to them brought a blessing in their lives, the fact that I served them after the spiritual manner could not fail to bring a blessing into my life.

A man lay dying in a prison hospital bed because he had not been sufficiently obedient to the laws and conditions of nutrition. He had worked for months in the prison bakeshop and got into the habit of subsisting almost exclusively on milk, toast and white sugar. The outcome was tuberculosis.

He had violated the law in a most unreasonable and flagrant way. Was I therefore to look upon him as bad through and through? Was I to dismiss him with, "You've made your bed; now lie in it"? Or, "You have what you deserve"? No. In spite of his action I was to see him as still good, and as one still subject to the Law of Good. I was to act after the manner of a man who is both righteous and merciful and by this act give birth to a man who could see God in the face of his afflicted patient. I was to demonstrate the second set of three Beatitudes, and by applying righteousness and mercy draw to me the vision to see the image of God in the personality of a dying man. I was to give recognition to my central position between two worlds. With one hand I was to reach up and take the hand of God. With the other I was to reach down and take the hand of my erring brother. And then permit the Kingdom to do the rest.

The patient got well. The prison doctor got the credit, which helped him by stimulating his faith in the treatment he prescribed. I gave the credit to God, which helped me in many ways. Everyone concerned was aided, and it was once more demonstrated that when God distributes His blessings He does so with a lavish hand.

In a prison hospital it is not easy to keep the peace, to retain the goodwill and friendship of your co-workers without alienating the sympathies of some. That I was enabled to do better than anyone else was due, to a large extent, to my Wednesday programme. I took literally the advice of Paul, "Bear ye one another's burdens, and so fulfil the law of Christ."

Usually I went to bed around seven in the morning and got up around one. My custom was to eat and then spend a couple of hours in the open air. On Wednesday, however, I would forgo this recreation and instead devote the afternoon to helping the day men with their various duties. In other words, I would share their burdens.

This was going "the other mile." In the cementing of needed friendships it was a most practical application of the law. For these favours were often returned to me when I was on duty at night. And I found a ready willingness on the part of my fellows to get up at a late hour in response to my call upon them for help in some emergency. Only friends are willing to do these things without even a suggestion of protest.

I found that love was the only obligation I had to meet in my work and associations; that the Apostle was correct when he said, "Owe no man anything, but to love one another; for he that loveth another hath fulfilled the law."

It is difficult to believe these great truths until after they have been demonstrated over and over. Most of us consider portions of Jesus' teachings as counsels of perfection, demanding too much from us and returning too little. Hence we are apt to practise some of them and ignore others as impossible and impractical.

During the years I've been outside I have found comparatively few persons who really believe non-resistance to evil is a workable teaching. Rather non-resistance is more likely to be condemned as weakness or a display of cowardice. Yet it is an invincible power when it is a genuine expression and not merely a respectable means of escaping the painful issues of evil.

Once an incoming patient, under the pressure of irritation, struck me without cause. We had our orders for dealing with all such incidents, and these orders did not involve non-resistance.

In a flash I inwardly forgave the man on the ground that he was not himself. In a flash too came the challenge from Jesus to do the hard thing, and to do it literally. "I say unto you, that you resist not evil: but whosoever shall smite thee on thy right cheek, turn to him the other also." Without a word I turned it, wholly surrendered to Christ, knowing not what would happen, nor caring. My attitude in the matter was, "The next thing to happen is the best thing." Whether struck again or not, I was the winner, mine was the victory and the profit, for I had done the hard thing, which was sneered at by those who lacked the courage to do it themselves. The current went out of the man. That helpless, unprotected other cheek had power to disarm him and to shame him. With a true contrite spirit he apologized and gave the reason for his temper. In that moment we became friends. We remained friends during my remaining time in prison, and for three years after I had been released we corresponded. That blow was the knock that opened the door of Christ for him. He serves Christ today.

Again I discovered in my Wednesday discipline that conformity to Divine Law out of fear of divine judgment paid far less dividends than did conformity which was a desire to evoke a love for law itself. Obeying the laws of man out of fear is better than breaking the laws. *But unless one obeys them out of love for them he cannot in the fullest sense be a law-abiding citizen. Neither, in the fullest sense, can he be a citizen of the spiritual world who fears the judgments of that world, and who obeys its laws out of fear instead of love.*

For many years I had hated all laws, manmade, natural, and divine. I had paid and paid for my disobedience. I decided I wanted to reverse this order. It has paid and paid in a better coin.

FOR THURSDAY: GOD'S INVINCIBILITY

God is Power

Ye shall receive power. —Acts 1:8.

The great power book, the Acts of the Apostles, the greatest power book of all literature, from beginning to end has been my joy in times of calm and fortress in times of storm. I have literally lived with the first two chapters. Nothing in all the sacred or profane writings now in existence can even remotely equal these two chapters. Every printed word in the world could be destroyed and humanity could struggle on. Destroy Acts 1 and 2 and the power source therein, and all civilized life on the planet would speedily crumble into the "Ruins of Empire."

Am I guilty of exaggeration? Not at all. For in these two chapters the eternal on-going and up-going are vouchsafed to man. Here is set forth the introduction of the third and never-ending Dispensation of God. Here the Power of the Holy Spirit is introduced and goes into action. Here for the first time in all human history the shackles are struck from the limbs of man, the power to rise is poured out, and the secret of individual and collective emancipation becomes available for all, male and female.

On Thursday I gave myself up to the study and practice of this power and the secret of its attainment. In the quiet of my own niche I would travel in imagination to that upper room and sit with that first group of spiritual pioneers, one hundred and twenty of them, waiting for the promise that for incredible ages had been the hope and the dream of a trapped humanity who could neither untie nor cut the knots of materialism which had bound them to an earth condition and had drugged the soul into helpless slumber. And here I would bathe myself in the mood of their patience and soak myself in the spirit of their unconquerable faith. Then I would read over and over again the secret of their attainment to power. And I would reflect upon the gigantic fact that they were willing to trust, to wait, "and not be tired by waiting."

I would permit myself to be convicted of impatience by their example, and I would bring to my remembrance the innumerable instances when I had forced things to happen prematurely, unwilling to let the right moment be born out of perfect ripeness, and to let the thing happen in exactly the right place and time. "And when the day of Pentecost was fully come…" The right moment, the ripe moment, the precise time for paying the cost for power and glory. "They were all with one accord in one place." The power came to them. And they were in a perfectly natural position: "they were sitting."

The Master had revealed the secret to them in advance. At this place they were applying it. That secret was "agreement." He had told them what it would mean if two would agree on earth, if two or three would gather in his name. If they could apply the secret of agreement, then so could I. The old lifer was the one with whom I agreed in prison. We were of one mind in one place. We made verses 1 and 2 of the second chapter of Acts have meaning and power for us.

So Thursday became a day of studying and applying the power of God through specific acts of agreement.

In prison was a man, Big Jeff by name, who had and maintained a reputation for fearlessness. He had a lot of *friends,* but no FRIENDS. His goodwill was cultivated by cowards who had no desire to attract his ill-will, and who found protection in the shadow of his dangerous notoriety.

Big Jeff was a problem for the prison officials, who found it necessary often to commit him to solitary confinement for his attacks on other prisoners and for his repeated attempts to escape. Punishment, however, had no good effect upon him, and his trend was from bad to worse. In time he developed an obsession in the form of an unreasonable suspicion. He was certain that he was constantly being plotted against by his enemies. To be caught glancing in his direction was to be marked for his anger. The officials knew that sooner or later he would attack the wrong man and they would have a nasty murder case on their hands. Big Jeff was placed in an isolation cell for his own protection and for the protection of other prisoners.

One day he struck a warder who opened his door. For this he was placed in solitary, and a short while later the thing happened to him that is the dread of every convict. He was moved to the hospital for observation before being tried and committed to an asylum for the criminally insane.

Both day and night reports on Big Jeff's actions and reactions were turned in to the warden. My own reports were always brief. Those of the day nurse were lengthy and full of trouble. Mine followed the same pattern with monotonous regularity, "Actions normal; reactions the same; slept well."

One morning as we were going off duty the night keeper in the hospital and I were called to the warden's office. When we arrived the warden was mulling over my reports on Big Jeff. He looked up and said, "I have information that you're leaving Big Jeff's door open every evening from seven to ten."

"There were no orders to the contrary," the warder replied.

"You should know better," said the warden. "He's under observation, isn't he? You should take it for granted that he's a menace to other patients; that you're to keep his door locked. This is the procedure during the day."

"I'll see to it hereafter," the warder affirmed.

"Of course I'm no stickler for hard and fast rules," the warden added. "I want my officers to show initiative and to act upon their own best judgment when it's warranted. I'm issuing no orders for or against closing the door. That's your responsibility."

I could almost see the warder smile inwardly.

"Thank you, warden," he said. "I shall accept it."

The warder was dismissed and I was asked to remain. The warden was interested in my reports on Big Jeff.

"The daytime reports and your night reports are just the opposite," he said. "How do you account for it?"

"The closed and open door," I replied. "That closed door in the daytime stands for fear of Jeff. It is matched by his behaviour. The open door at night stands for just the opposite. The result you know."

"Quite a theory," said the warden, "but I'm afraid it'll be a long while before it's adopted generally," he added, smiling. Then he asked bluntly: "Just what is your opinion of Big Jeff? What is the matter with him anyway?"

"Fear, warden," I replied.

"Fear!" he exclaimed. "Why, he's the most fearless man we've ever had in here."

"His fearlessness is a sham, warden," I said. "He's not afraid of physical pain. His fear lies deeper. It's psychic."

"How do you know that?" he asked.

"Because I had the same kind of fear for twenty years. It made a rebel of me. I didn't fear anything that man could do to me. What I feared was not actual or real. It was a shadow shape. Jeff is not insane. He's afraid down inside of him. Where this fear is there is torment. That's Big Jeff's trouble, warden, torment."

"We'll keep him over there for a while longer," the warden said. "If you can find this so-called fear you're talking about, do it. If there's anything you can do for him, do that."

I didn't care what Big Jeff's fear was. In the kind of treatment I applied the cause of his condition made no difference. All that was unknown to me I turned over to God and the transforming power of the Holy Spirit, which I was practising every day generally, on every Thursday particularly. For my own part in the treatment went into action after the manner of Peter's three great rules of "'stablish, strengthen, settle you."

Would the application of these rules to Big Jeff set him free? Yes, providing I had the capacity to *be* the rules in my own life. If in connection with Big Jeff I could be established in a genuine faith, strengthened in works of faith, and be settled in love for the tormented man, he could be unbound, released. I knew this.

On this problem the warder and I had a mutual interest. We discussed it together, and we came to a mutual agreement that Big Jeff was beyond the corrective powers of man, and therefore, in his case, God alone had the answer, the power, the correction. Upon this point we were absolutely of one mind.

Agreeing, we could ask in terms of action and it would be done unto us. We asked for Big Jeff's liberation in those terms of action.

First, we had faith in God's power and trust in Big Jeff's true self, his better nature, his inherent goodness. Second, we expressed the strength of our faith in works. We backed our faith up in actual works.

We opened wide his door. Third, we were settled in a genuine sympathy or love for him. And this was the way it worked out, unscientific and strangely theoretical though it may seem.

To our faith Big Jeff reacted true to the law of faith. He did not disappoint our established faith, nor did he betray our works of faith by taking advantage of an open door to do harm to others or to attempt escape. Since torment comes out of fear, and since love is the quality of God's power that casts out fear, we not only opened Big Jeff's door, but we invited him out to spend the evening hours in the hall and convalescent room.

He was then invited to help me minister to my patients, actually to perform missions of service, mercy, love for others, even to the reading of stories to some of the more helpless ones.

The days went into weeks. Our night-time example with Big Jeff was copied by the daytime staff. Jeff became as familiar about the hospital as were the attendants. At times he would accompany the doctor on his morning rounds, amending and carrying the record charts. At others he would help with the taking of temperatures.

In these weeks of ministering to the needs of others the restricted area of Jeff's love life was slowly opened up. And when it had been sufficiently opened up it banished the cause and fact of his torment. He served out his sentence as a model prisoner and was released to become a credit to the society he had once preyed upon.

In practising the power of God, as in practising all His other attributes, I had a passion for His challenge to "Prove me." I found it was more valuable to apply God's word to my own life and to the lives of others than it was to remain apart in the academic study of His word or of the systems and doctrines men had built up around Him. I wanted to know about Him, of course; but I preferred to get this theology by actual experience, by learning of Him "down among men." I had a conviction that God would work in all the areas and affairs of my life if I would let Him work. This conviction I still possess.

In the experience of my wife and myself we have been confronted with many severe human problems rising out of a mistaken diagnosis of what are spiritual and what merely psychic phenomena. There are certain sensitive and aspiring temperaments for whom "signs and wonders" hold a luminous and treacherous fascination. They sometimes wind up as *saviours* of the world via the destruction of the world. They speak of having a *message,* and they refer mysteriously to some vague personality beyond the mundane sense of sight, who has singled them out of the multitude to be crowned with his own halo and adorned with his own ethereal wings. They have become his *chosen vessel* for the purification of the race. It seems to make little difference to their own purification, for as the message *comes through,* the trend of their own lives turns towards the grotesque and the freakish in workaday conduct and religious behaviour.

A few years ago a woman who had been a devotee of the wrong kind of message came to our home for counsel. Her plunge down had been quick and devastating. From a trim, efficient, and beautiful secretary she had become a decrepit old woman, mumbling incoherently about a blind world that refused to listen to her warning and refused to accept the salvation offered it by her *guide* from the other side.

She was afflicted in all the areas of her personality. From a practical standpoint she was an abject failure. Her health was gone. Her emotions were destructive. Her mind was feeble. She was in complete poverty. She was utterly antisocial. She was devoid of any moral stamina. And she was in complete captivity to spiritual inertia.

Before her all the bulwarks of mental science went down. Upon this point my wife and I agreed that insofar as the power of man was concerned this woman was absolutely hopeless. That was the negative agreement. Now came the positive agreement. We agreed in the truism that "man's extremity is God's opportunity." We agreed that with God nothing was impossible, not even the rehabilitation of this woman's life.

With this agreement as a basis for intercession the woman was released into God's hands. This was followed by the application of faith in her better nature. And this was followed by actual works of faith, tangible assistance for her and actual attention given to her creature needs. There was an active and spontaneous love for her, a vast and uninterrupted sympathy.

One day she said voluntarily, the old light of reason and intelligence in her eyes, "I read the Bible last night for the first time in three years. I was reading in the Book of Acts about Pentecost. Suddenly I felt that I had been on the wrong path. Then I felt a confidence in myself, and a power I had never known before. I went to bed and slept the night through without a single dream and vision. When I woke this morning I knew I had been healed."

She had never spoken truer words in her life.

A young girl, caught in the same kind of trap, came to our home one afternoon. My wife was away, and I was busy typing in a little study back of our house. The girl heard my typewriter and sat down on the lawn-swing to wait. On the swing was the Bible, opened at the Book of Acts. Beside it was a bunch of my pencilled notes. To pass the time while waiting for me to finish my work, she began to look up and read the references I had jotted down. The first one struck her as being especially suited to her own need, "I am with thee and no man shall set on thee to hurt thee." Acts 19:10. She turned to Acts 7:9. "God was with him and delivered him out of all his afflictions." Then, "It shall be told thee what thou must do." Acts 9:6.

At this moment I got up from my work, went out and found the girl. I listened while she told me her story. When she had finished I asked her to open the Bible at random and place her finger on a passage. I didn't know exactly why I told her this. It was not my usual mode of giving advice. She put her finger on Ecclesiastes 8:5. "Whoso keepeth the commandments shall feel no evil thing." She was told to repeat the act. She got the 121st Psalm, verse 2. "My help cometh from the Lord who made heaven and earth." Again she was told to seek. This time she put her finger on Psalm 91:11. "For He shall give His angels charge over thee, to keep thee in all thy ways."

Three times God had spoken directly to her and for her difficulty. She came under the heavy poundage of a dark weight. She left convinced of her future course and the divine protection. In other words, her problem had been solved, the seed for her complete healing planted.

Those prison Thursdays, given up exclusively to the practice of the power of God, were a delight and a light to me. When people inquire about spiritual power, without hesitation, I reply with the Book of Acts.

FOR FRIDAY: THE SERENITY OF GOD

God is Peace

Peace I leave with you; my peace I give unto you: not as the world giveth, give I unto you. —John 14:27.

The seventh Beatitude revealed to me that God is Peace and that the peacemaker is a son of God. I discovered that peace was an interior quality, reflecting from the inside out and not from the outside in. In the cultivation of this peace, however, I learned that it could be established within by reflecting on outer scenes. Friday, therefore, was devoted to the art and practice of peace by means of reflection, and by means of seeking the inner silence.

I am thankful that I had my start in the pursuits of peace while I was in prison. Here my attention was not divided by the alarms so prevalent among the teachers and counsellors of the outside world. Since coming out of prison I have found that most people regard the cultivation of silence as incompatible with the practical designs for living. It is thought of as belonging to the plane of mystical philosophy and esoteric science, having no utilitarian value, but much of utilitarian danger. In most of the student circles with which I have come in contact, a silence-seeker and an ascetic are one and the same thing. A person who follows a discipline of silence, the culture of inner peace, is often looked upon as a recluse or a hermit, who is practically useless in the world, and who frequently exhibits *queer* traits of character.

I suppose there are such persons; but I doubt the claim that the subject of peace is responsible for their abnormalities. My own experience teaches me that no one can pursue peace in vain, nor reap from the pursuit anything but beneficial results. A peacemaker is one who has the peace of God in his heart. A person who does not possess this inner peace is no peacemaker, and under no circumstances nor by the widest stretch of the imagination is he fit to make peace. A peacemaker makes peace by what he is and not by what he claims to be. By having peace within himself he establishes peace around himself. In his presence peace is felt. The peacemaker is ever the normal person. The noise-maker is ever abnormal, and from the spiritual point of view, he is a pathological case. He pursues the actuality of noise to escape the reality of poise. Sound and fury always signify nothing. Peace is Reality, and Reality has menace only for unreality.

When the subject is inner peace the alarms of reflection vanish. The culture of silence is, to me, a surrender to God, the finest and noblest surrender of all, and it is the most productive of personal and collective good. From a purely practical standpoint, I am aware of no discipline that will return more rounded profits to its devotees.

The efficient and persistent cultivation of peace leads to the illuminative life. It does release the interior energies of the soul and deeper mind. It brings mental illumination and the inspired intellect. It sets interior powers and capacities free, as nothing else will. Of course, if having tasted the serenity and bliss of the released soul, a person decides to feed on the heavenly manna without concern for the actual world, he will inevitably come to grief. He will lose the radiance he has found, a gloom will settle upon his personal spirit, and he will become a victim to the most intolerable condition known to man, physical and spiritual inertia, both present at one and the same time. This is the zero of despair. In the East it is called "The dark night of the soul."

To be safe one need only take the example and promise of Jesus. He was in possession of the illumined mind and the peaceful heart. He was ever passive to God and positive to man, a perfect balance of passivity and positivity. To follow this example is to avoid the penalties of error. The Occidental world has missed the mark in that it is positive both to God and man. The Oriental world has missed the mark in that it is passive both to God and man. Neither has caught the balance, and both have paid the penalty, and will continue to pay the penalty for this error. They will both continue to "cry peace, and there is no peace." Jesus had the mountaintop experience of peace at all times. But he did not employ the gift towards selfish ends. He came down from the high altitudes of the spirit and wrestled positively with the problems of men: "My peace I give unto you. Let not your heart be troubled, neither let it be afraid." He shared all that he possessed. He did not clutch it to himself, for by this method was it lost. By sharing it, was it retained. There will be no "dark night of the soul" if the seeker after the inner peace will copy this example.

After my dungeon experience I took to *silence* as the duck takes to water. I had no misgivings about it. No fears, no anxieties. I knew that the oil of anxiety and the water of peace could not mix. So I stood with Paul, "In nothing be anxious; but in everything by prayer and supplication with thanksgiving let your request be made known unto God." After reading the scripture I had no doubt but that anxiety and doubt of God were one and the same. I could not trust God and entertain anxiety at the same time, but I could give my anxiety to God in return for His peace. Or as Peter says, "Casting all your anxiety upon Him, because He careth for you."

I discovered in practice that if I could become anxious over one of my patients and could then cast my anxiety upon God, really and completely let go of it, that peace would come in its place, not only to me but to my patient as well, resulting more often than not in a thorough and permanent healing.

For this Friday programme I found it helpful to have a peace Bible at hand, compiled by myself. Reading this Bible helped to establish the mood and atmosphere of peace, which had a quieting effect on my patients, often inspiring hope in them as surely as an atmosphere of confusion would arouse despair and doubt. The ill are keenly sensitive to the mood, the thoughts and feelings of those around them, and are reinforced or depleted accordingly. For me to carry an air of worry and irritation among my patients was equal to carrying obscene literature to impressionable youths, or drugs to weak men. To walk among my patients with an atmosphere of uncertainty, doubt, confusion, and fear was not only wicked, but it was to commit a psychological crime upon them. The reading of my peace Bible did much to ward off the commission of this criminal act upon the helpless. Too, this peace reading from authorized sources inspired me and justified me in the pursuits of my own inner sanctuary of peace.

I had no more time than other people to practise the peace culture. My prison night was twelve hours long. My duties stretched from six to six, and there were two full floors of hospital patients, always a large number of them being bedridden and requiring constant observation and attention. I was the only nurse on duty at night. I had neither an assistant nor an orderly. I had to snatch my periods for practice between calls.

Yet the one objection I most hear to the practice of silence is that it is a luxury possible only to the idle, to those who can afford to fill in their vast leisure with long forages into the contemplative existence. If this objection fails, there is the old reliable "bugaboo" to fall back on, the timeworn "view with alarm" counsel to shy away from silence, lest you fall into a trance and "get deluded" on psychic manifestations. I have no instance in my memory where the peace of Jesus resulted in psychic or other illusory results.

Obviously the world is crowded with deluded dabblers in psychic phenomena. But these are anything but peace-seekers or peacemakers, and they experience anything but spiritual truth.

My own experiences have been salutary. They have not made me less but more practical; not less but more capable as a social being.

In silence, different energies are released. Some have a negative and some a positive influence. All are dynamic and have the power to alter the expression of life, to change the body chemistry and the normal mood.

There is the dynamic silence that falls between two friends at the point of saying goodbye. So great is the power of this silence that it renders them speechless. If speech is forced it falls flat, empty, dry, inane. It is sterile and awkward, and only serves to emphasize the silence in command of the situation. Feelings are released at this moment which defy expression through speech. And there is usually an urge to mask these feelings with sham smiles and lively nonsense.

There is the dynamic silence of an empty chair at the table, of a house after a funeral. The silence of two lovers after their first quarrel. The silence of parents waiting for the doctor to come out. The deepening of this silence just before his verdict. There is the silence of a mother as she reads the casualty list in the newspaper, or sits listening to it over the radio. The silence of an old lady knitting, of an old man reading his Bible. The silence in a courtroom as the jury files in. The silence of a prison just before the zero hour for someone to walk the last mile. There is the silence of a disappointed trust, of a sudden and unexpected hurt. There is the silence of guilt, of shame. The silence of the still, cold face of a dear one, crowded with the memories of his or her loving services. There is the silence that comes with contrition over a neglected one who is now beyond the sting of loneliness. All these silences have power to affect the even course of life.

Often in the practice of peace I would call upon memory, recapture and reflect upon peaceful scenes. A certain summer night remembered and now relived would evoke the mood of peace. The memory of a country road or lane, or a country churchyard! A certain springtime Sabbath morning with its indescribable peacefulness and contentment, its bright warm hush, its contagious lull! The interior of a certain church on a certain day! The memory of coming upon a nun at prayer! An old man in his garden! Two sweethearts in the moonlight! The memory of a still forest, a cool grassy valley, a shaded pool! All or any of these memories had power to woo me away from inner confusion and back to my centre of peace.

Often, too, I would make use of the much-maligned daydream in my search for the inner quiet. I would reflect upon things as my fancy would have them be and not as they were in the cold glare of actuality. I would see the world at peace. I would see men remove their masks of greed and hate and put on the Image of love and selflessness. I would see the causes of suffering eliminated, poverty, crime, and war banished. In my day-dreams I would remake the world and re-people it with congenial spirits who lived for and not against each other. I would see Christ-like men at the head of things, pointing the way by their example. Through these reveries I could lure myself back to thoughts of "quietness and confidence."

Also, I would imitate peaceful things and peaceful persons. A picture of Edison at his work, relaxed, lost in his task! The serene smile on the face of one whose spirit had departed! A sleeping child limp on a pillow! A cat among friends asleep on the floor! These imitations had a way of letting out tension and letting in peace.

In peace power is generated. In action it is expressed. I would remind myself of this often. When I would become caught in the vortex of confusion I would recall that my real *I* dwelt in the centre of eternal peace and harmony. And I would quote 1 Corinthians 14: 33 mentally, "For God is not the author of confusion, but of peace," or Mark 4:39, "Peace, be still."

And getting peace within myself I would walk softly among my patients, letting that peace do its perfect work.

In prison the eyesight easily becomes impaired. Farsightedness is a common condition among prisoners. It is mostly due to accumulated tensions. Once these have been relaxed the eyesight usually becomes normal once more.

A young man who was going blind was committed to the hospital for a general rundown condition. His nerves were taut, and he seemed unable to relax. He slept drawn up in a knot, clutching the bed, his face pressed tight into his pillow. He could not properly digest his food, nor assimilate it.

I would seek and find peace within myself and then I would find occasion to be around him. At night I would step into his room while he slept and let my peaceful state affirm for him, "Thou wilt keep him in perfect peace." Often before my eyes the tensions would go out of his body and he would pass from restless sleep into peaceful slumber.

In time, without instruction, the peace habit became so permanently integrated into his consciousness that he was healed of tension. With the healing his eyesight was restored.

Peace around an ill person has very great therapeutic value. But with the release of peace within an ill person there is almost certain to occur liberated energies whose nature it is to re-create and heal. An institution for the mentally ill whose staff was dedicated to the practice and establishment of peace would give the world some important discoveries and set a far-reaching example. This prophetic statement I base upon many pages out of my own experience.

I have followed many progressive self-applied methods for the establishment of inner peace. The following one of seven progressive steps I have found effective. I used it during my prison days, and have used it ever since. In their order the steps are:

1. Releasing tensions.
2. Spiritual subject.
3. Fixation of attention.
4. Prayer.

5. Meditation.
6. Silence.
7. Gratitude.

The feeling of gratitude is a spontaneous reaction if the steps preceding have been done proficiently and successfully. For so joyous a state of tranquillity one must automatically feel grateful. At least I have found it so.

FOR SATURDAY: THE SOURCE OF JOY

God is Joy

The joy of the Lord is your strength. —Nehemiah 8:10.

It may not be precisely accurate to say God is joy, but there is plenty of scriptural evidence to support the assertion that He is the Source of Joy, which amounts to about the same thing.

"Wherefore I perceive that there is nothing better than that a man should rejoice in his works, for that is his portion."

"Ye shall rejoice in all that ye put your hand to."

"The joy of the Lord is your strength."

"Delight thyself also in the Lord, and He shall give thee the desires of thine heart."

"Therefore God, even thy God, hath anointed thee with the oil of gladness above all thy fellows."

"These things have I spoken unto you in order that I may have joy in you, and that your joy may become perfect."

"Be glad and rejoice."

"Behold I bring you good tidings of great joy."

How often do we yield to the temptation to think of Jesus as "A man of sorrow, and acquainted with grief." We forget that He was also a man of gladness and acquainted with joy.

The Value of Training

Saturday was a day set aside especially for the practice of joy. This was a day for making a special effort to make others happy. Dr. Glenn Clark put his finger on a miracle-working truth when he advised the woman, *"Don't try to change him: try to make him happy."* For therein lies the key to a great many problems. Seldom if ever can we make others happy by trying to change them to suit our own designs. And if they are not happy about our efforts they certainly are not going to be changed for the better, but for the worse.

Our chaplain was holding up some religious reading matter of mine without a reasonable cause, I thought. I could have thrown a brain storm about it. I could have taken it over his head to the warden in an effort to make him change his mind. Had I done so and gained this one point, the chaplain was in a position to make things difficult in all manner of other directions for me. Instead I found a couple of ways to make him happy, without his knowing the source of this happiness. He voluntarily and with the utmost goodwill lifted his ban and gave me the books.

A patient who refused to cooperate with the day nurse and would not take a prescribed treatment of medicine was put under force. The nurse sought to make him take it by threatening him. For this the nurse nearly lost his job. I was less foolish. For when I came on duty and encountered the man's stubbornness, I did not try to change his mind, but set about to devise ways for making him happy. He capitulated to the treatment.

A man who was the irritation and thorn-in-the-flesh to the hospital attendants had only been made worse by their forcing methods. I found a crippled baby sparrow for him to care for. It made him happy and it changed his life.

A mother came to our house to issue a long complaint against her adolescent daughter. "I'm at my wit's end," she said. "She won't do a thing I want her to do. She does just the reverse."

"Stop worrying and nagging and trying to force her," we replied, "and devote yourself to making her happy. Let your joy be found in this action, and not in the hope of results."

Since there was nothing else to do she took the advice. A short while later she reported that the girl seemed to have changed overnight.

Another woman came for help on a problem that had not yet happened. "If my daughter takes up drinking and smoking," she said, "I'll simply die."

"Have you told the girl that?" we asked.

"Indeed I have, many times," she affirmed. "And I mean it."

"And the girl hasn't taken up drink and cigarettes?"

"No; but I'm worried sick for fear she will."

"You have not threatened enough. The girl has a strong character. It will take a lot of your suspicion, mistrust, worry, and threats to ruin your daughter. It can be done, however, and the chances are ten to one it will be, unless you set about to trust her and to make her happy to be your daughter."

She refused the advice. The girl took to drink, smoking, and night life, and finally ran away with a paroled prisoner, married him, committed a crime with him and got herself arrested.

The mother didn't die, but lived on to say, "I told you so."

With babies the best results are obtained, not by forcing them, but by making them happy. Put a rope around a dog's neck and its first reaction is to pull against you. If you pull you have made an enemy of the dog at the outset. You may cow it and by breaking its spirit get your way and thus train it to the leash. But if when the dog pulls you yield, it too will soon yield. Thus you have trained the dog without breaking its spirit or sacrificing its spontaneous friendship.

It pays to practise the way of joy.

Things done in joy are easily done and well done. The first draft of a story is often the best draft, though it rarely comes up to literary standards in form. It is easily done, because it is done with the energy of creative joy, and this joy is transmitted to the reader. In the absence of joy, labour may creep into revision and weigh heavily upon the reader. Jesus did his work in joy, and thus he could proclaim the easiness of his yoke and the lightness of his burden.

First to rise to the elevation of joy and then pick up the task, is the light and burdenless way. To remain under the task and force it up is the hard way, the laborious, the drudging way, the sweat-of-the-brow way of the Old Testament.

A father came to talk over the problem of his young son who was drifting toward bad associations.

"What's your son worth to you?" he was asked.

"Everything I've got and myself with it," he said.

"Including a chunk of your time?" he was asked.

"I see what you mean," he replied.

"Give some Sundays over to making him happy. Go to the mountains. Be with him man to man. Pal with him. Take time out to consult him about your own affairs. Adventure with him. Make him glad and he'll not disappoint your hopes."

In the process the father discovered he had been missing a lot of joy himself. He didn't have to worry about his son's associates any more.

It was good and beneficial practice for me to specialize in the joyous life one day out of seven; to cultivate the habit of rejoicing in the happiness I could bring to others. I found it well worthwhile to reserve one day for the practice of God's presence *in the pursuit of His joys.*

CHAPTER 19

MY NEW NAME

THE LIFER ONCE SUGGESTED THAT I LEAVE PRISON WITH A NEW name. Such a possibility had not occurred to me. Sometime later, while discussing the psychological effect that certain names had on certain personalities, he told me that a name could often make or break a man. He added that a name had the power both to impress the mind and motivate the heart at one and the same time—all of which was more or less vague to me then. I was destined to learn by experience of the tremendous influence a name could have on the conduct and behaviour of a human being.

From time to time I thought of what he had said, but my interest in a new name was not sufficient to set me out upon the quest for it. During my criminal career I had had many different names, and they had all brought me to the same dead-end passage, through the winding and twisting paths of crime to the big iron gates of prison. Perhaps this had something to do with my lack of interest now. Anyway, his suggestion apparently failed to register, for the idea of assuming another name soon dropped out of my consciousness.

Quite some time had elapsed, during which I had taken up a correspondence course of short story writing. One of the lessons in the course had to do with visualization, its practice and development. The lesson fascinated me, and I soon found it comparatively easy for me to see with my mind's eye the pictures and actions of my imagination. Suddenly my newly acquired proficiency in the art of visualizing ceased abruptly.

I had cut a picture out of a magazine, a young mother sitting beside a baby-crib. With this as a starting-point, I began to imagine a series of motives and consistent actions involving the woman and her child. Then I sat down to visualize these actions. But no sooner had I closed my eyes than my purpose seemed to vanish from my thoughts, and a visual design entirely foreign to the purpose presented itself to my mind's eye.

At first I paid little or no attention to this interference, but when, later on, I sat down to try my exercise again and the same design appeared to defeat me, I began to wonder about it. This wonder drifted into a downright sense of curiosity when, after the passage of many hours, I tried once more with the same result.

After three days of having my purposes thwarted by this mental kind of whim, or whatever it was, a definite feeling of annoyance took possession of me. This became exasperation when the thing began even to haunt me in my sleep, seeming to keep me in a half-awake condition all through the night. The design was composed of two objects: a sun just half over the horizon, and above it a five-pointed star.

I had passed through four different stages of reaction before mentioning the phenomenon to the lifer—wonder, curiosity, exasperation, and finally alarm.

"It's your new name," the old lifer said simply. "Tomorrow evening I'll see if I can't help you to understand it better."

On the following evening he informed me that he had had a friend draw the design for him. He unrolled a piece of wrapping paper showing the design and tacked it on his working board. I got down beside him, and with the object before us, he began to explain just what it was all about.

"The sun," he said, "indicates day. Now what does the star above it indicate?"

I was eager to find out.

"Wouldn't it seem to indicate a daily star?"

"Yes," I agreed.

"Suppose we transpose the words," he suggested. "Then we would have star daily. Now suppose this were to be used as a proper name, thus—" And he printed below the design the two words, Starr Daily. "See!" He beamed. "Simple, isn't it? That's your new moniker, boy. Good one, too. Got a lot of meaning and power in it. Lot o' dangerous dynamite, also." Suddenly he grew sober.

"It means a way of life, son, a daily shining. But don't forget, the sun is just halfway over the horizon. That indicates that it can be a setting as well as a rising sun. If you fail to live up to the high meaning of the name the sun will sink below the horizon. Make a heroic effort and it will rise. It's up to you which way your sun will go."

He then took a coin from his pocket and placed it in the centre of the star, and by this means traced a circle. In this circle he printed the word SPIRIT. Just above the top point he printed the word MORAL. The right upper point he thus designated MENTAL; the lower right point, FINANCIAL; the lower left point, PHYSICAL; and the upper left point, SOCIAL. These he called the primary areas of my human personality.

Each of them was to be developed in an entirely new way, and none was to be developed at the expense of another. I was here taught my greatest lesson on the methodology of *Surrender*.

I was not, for instance, to develop my moral area by drawing solely upon the will power resident in my mental area; but was to employ that will power to direct my moral weaknesses to the centre. In other words, to surrender them to SPIRIT utterly and without compromise and thus permit SPIRIT to do ITS perfect work with them, absorb and transform them according to SPIRIT'S unfailing Law of Love.

I would need intellectual development. But again this was not to be accomplished at the expense of other areas composing my personality; at the expense of my health, for example, or at the expense of social balance and efficiency. I was to surrender my intellect to SPIRIT, dedicate it to the SPIRIT'S will, and let SPIRIT have ITS perfect way as a director and developer of my intellectual capacities, according to SPIRIT'S unfailing Law of Love.

I would not labour by the sweat of my brow in order to possess myself of those things needful to my financial environment, for to gain economic emancipation in this manner would be detrimental to other areas of my personality; mind and body, for instance. But I would surrender all these needs to SPIRIT, and let SPIRIT have ITS perfect way in directing me toward the fulfilling of my creature necessities, according to SPIRIT'S unfailing Law of Love.

Nor would I seek to maintain my physical health and vigour at the expense of my mental area by wasting endless hours on planned health regimens, exercises, diets, and the like; but I would surrender all this to my centre, SPIRIT, and let SPIRIT have ITS perfect way in directing me concerning diet, exercise, play, work, according to SPIRIT'S unfailing Law of Love.

And lastly I would not struggle with my antisocial habits at the expense of my mental and nervous system. I would surrender this problem to SPIRIT, and let SPIRIT have ITS perfect way in the elimination of my timidities and superiorities, according to SPIRIT'S unfailing Law of Love.

In other words, I would seek ever to draw upon spiritual energy for all my personality needs and thus get an even distribution of power over the five areas of my personality.

Such is the history and analysis of my new name. The lifer brought scripture to bear upon this lesson, and he, himself, was an example of the development with which he tried to acquaint me. For he certainly had attained a high degree of emancipation.

All five of his primary personality areas were dedicated to one purpose, that of letting the central light of SPIRIT shine through him and use him according to the Supreme Law of Love.

CHAPTER 20

AFTER PRISON, WHAT?

U NDER THIS HEAD MAUD BALLINGTON BOOTH PUBLISHED A book many years ago. It dealt with matters accumulated out of her long experience in prison and social work. The book, while widely read by convicts, was not charitably received by them. It exploited society's negative attitude toward the convict, but I fear its contribution was to the convict's weakness rather than his strength.

In this final chapter I have no desire to whitewash society. But I do have a desire to state emphatically that society's attitude toward convicts and ex-convicts is but a natural reaction. If a man has been genuinely healed of his criminal personality, the reaction of society toward him is uniformly gracious and helpful. But if he comes out of prison with only a head full of good intentions, and with a heart still capable of seizing the slightest excuse for committing crime, he will promptly be given that excuse. Society will consistently mistrust him, and the representatives of the law will hound and often aggravate him. But I have found in my own experience that no such excuses are offered the man who comes out of prison endowed with a true desire to serve society rather than to prey upon it.

No man ever came out of prison at a more inopportune time than I did. In March, 1930, when my sentence came to an end, I faced a world at the peak of depression. There simply were no jobs to be had in a world in which the most capable men and women were willing to work for their keep in order to avoid charity. Millions of the unemployed roamed the streets and the country. Against this universal opposition, one would think that an ex-convict who had scarcely earned an honest dollar in his life, who had nothing to recommend him but a long, black criminal record, would find the odds against success entirely too great to be overcome.

Foreseeing this problem, the lifer helped to build in me the right attitude for meeting my panic-torn world. *If I could leave prison, not with just the usual good intentions motivated by fear of further punishment, but with a real spontaneous desire to be of service to society and the human race, I should never be hounded by the law, and society would seek and find me and would offer more opportunities than I could ever embrace.*

"No man can rub himself out," he said, "without letting God in. If God is in the picture or pattern of your life, He'll find plenty for you to do. Those deprived and suffering millions out there have surrendered to the wrong deity."

From this point of vantage, my greatest riddle is that people can lack the perception to trust God in their economic as well as their spiritual affairs.

"Never seek to obtain anything through self-planned contact," the old lifer said. No wiser statement has ever fallen from purely human lips upon my ears. In these years of freedom, I have departed from that sage advice scores of times. Not once have I succeeded. Nor have I ever sought an end through self-conceived and self-planned human contact that my integrity did not become involved in some form or other of deception, false tact, or insincere diplomacy.

At last I have learned that, for me at least, the only contacts worth embracing are those which God plans and executes. Against all others shines a big red light or the yellow light of caution. I know now that God's light is green, and that when I get this light I have an unerring divine guidance to move. Not once in these years has that green light failed me. Hundreds of contacts have been made for me by God and in no case of this kind has my integrity ever been involved, in no instance have I had to employ deception or use an insincere diplomacy or tact in order to remove resistance standing in the way of my aims.

I have gone against the green light of God's guidance by not waiting for it. Many times I have done this in my lecture work, but in no such case have I had God's power and inspiration to sustain me. Instead I have had to labour by the sweat of my brow in order to remove audience resistance and to capture attention. I mean by this that I have been forced back upon psychological methods of salesmanship to remove resistance, and this has always violated the integrity of my soul. On the other hand, when I have gone before my audience under God's guidance, empty, child-like, fine enough to be used by God's power, the resistance has been removed even before I mounted the platform. When God does the thing, He does it right. When man does it in the absence of God, he is compelled to labour in competition with opposing forces. Thus his very success is failure, and what is more, his deeper self tells him so. No man could ever fail in anything on the basis of the Golden Rule, providing the Golden Rule and the man were one and the same thing.

When I began to contemplate the day of my release, and to consider the new attitude of going out to serve rather than to exploit society, the idea of developing some special talent presented itself. I asked the lifer what I should take up in this connection. He advised me to make a list of all the things I could think of in the way of serviceable talents. This I did. Then he told me to study my long list, and when I had found the hardest thing on it, to make that my choice.

This was somewhat confusing, for I had unwittingly put down some things, which under the circumstance of prison conditions were impossible of development.

"Nothing you have on the list is impossible," he said.

"They are all talents. They are all potential within you. The fact that you thought of putting them down is an evidence of this. Pick out the hardest one, and then listen to God's challenge to 'stir up the talent within you.'"

"But why start with the hardest?" I asked. "A baby has to learn to walk."

"And wear rompers," he added, facetiously. "You're old enough for pants. The hardest things to do are always of the greatest social good. And the greatest opposition always releases the greatest power. Think of Christ's opposition and His power."

I had put down on the list the talent of writing for publication. Since I had no education to amount to anything, and since the only writing a convict was allowed to do for outside consumption was his weekly or biweekly letter, I was compelled to choose this as the hardest thing on my list, for it stood as an impossibility from my point of view.

Before leaving prison I wrote for magazines, and I have written for them ever since. To this talent has been added its sister, public speaking, and with these two outlets God has seen fit to keep me busy.

I know there are hundreds of men and women in prison who want to know the will of God for them. To these I would leave this parting message:

Though the world does not know it, your prison cell offers you your greatest opportunity right now for self-improvement. Depart from the common practice of "doing" time, and embrace the practice of "using" time, cultivate the attitude of "give" and turn away from the attitude of "get" and you will come to the end of your stretch with God on your side. If your release from prison is endorsed by Christ, and you enter your new life with no indispensable sponsor save God, yours will be a life of service, protection, and the only happiness that is worth a dime, that which comes from victory over your own lesser self by allowing the love of your greater self to have release. I can say this to you with a sense of authority. The contents of this book are my testimony and my proof.

EPILOGUE

ON MORE THAN A SCORE OF OCCASIONS I WAS PERMITTED TO hear what in my opinion constituted preeminent discussions on crime and criminals. These were carried on between the lifer and our visiting priest, who was most commonly known to all convicts as Father Good, a name which expressed the universal esteem in which the aged cleric was held.

From these discussions one point stood out clear and promising: in the prison system society had its best opportunity to make a large and lasting contribution to the social order; and religion inside of prison walls had its best opportunity to render missionary service after the programme of a living Christ.

The lifer and Father Good, men of learning and experience, always presented their views on the modern prison system against a background of failure. In this they were ever supported by the cold, hard figures in the record. Through the twenty-five years of my own prison experience, save for the First World War period, I at no time observed a decrease in the prison population, or in the national cost of crime. Due to the steady increase in criminal laws and the gradual shifting of moral and conventional poles, the popularity of gangster films and fiction, the detailed and dramatized accounts of crime in the newspapers and over the radio, the corruption in politics, the cultivation of the world-owes-me-a-living attitude in the school system, the steady softening of body, mind, and conscience in a mechanized age—these and many more factors have made the increase in crime inevitable and, with our present equipment, its decrease impossible.

"Religion," said Father Good, "is Democracy's only hope of survival. The state can never be stronger than the religion under it. When the religious supports decay, licence becomes the rule for those fundamental principles upon which a democratic government is based. A man whose conscience has become blunted in the absence of religious convictions will misuse the principle of free speech, of free press, of free worship, and of free assemblage. An irreligious society is the breeding ground for crime. The end for such a society is criminal rule."

In the light of today, these remarks bear a singular aptness.

According to this old priest, then, the first approach to the crime problem is in society itself. The demand here is a return to prayer and to God. Without these the human conscience sags, a fact well known even to the atheist Voltaire, who said, "If there were no God it would be necessary to invent one."

During my last two and one-half years in prison I canvassed several hundred convicts concerning their religious background. With monotonous regularity I was told there had been no such background. Only an occasional one could remember any prayer life in his home; only a comparatively few had ever seen a Bible in the home; only now and then did I find a man who could recall having heard the name of God or Christ spoken in the home, except where these sacred names had been taken in vain. But, like me, many of those questioned could remember strong religious impulses in their childhood lives, impulses which were kept secret because of a warning instinct which told them that any such expression would be met with silent contempt or hurtful ridicule.

In the face of an unregenerate society, according to Father Good and the lifer, the prison system at best was greatly handicapped. But since the religious impulse was in man, however overlaid with the crust of crime, that system could be made effective by the introduction of a vigorous prison religion. They both felt that a genuine system of prison religion would prevent a large percentage of first offenders from becoming old offenders, and that it would greatly reduce the ranks of the habitual criminal population.

To them an effective prison system would be based upon a three-point programme: physical, mental, and spiritual.

They both agreed that criminality was a disease of the conscience. This disease was not inherited, but a predisposition to it was inheritable. The early environment of the child had much to do with the development of the predisposed criminal tendencies. If such an environment was deficient in religious practice, the progressive blunting of the conscience was almost a foregone conclusion. A prison environment without an adequate religious practice only added sledge hammer blows to a conscience already battered beyond recognition. In other words, an effective prison system would supply the environment which had not been supplied in the home.

Those who come into the world predisposed toward crime will nearly always, upon close examination, reflect it in their physical and nervous organisms. There may be a physical inadequacy, an immaturity in the reproductive parts, which makes them secretive and sensitive, fearful and inferior. In prison this immediately becomes a constant source of anxiety. The weekly shower with its consequent exposure of their immaturities keeps them overshadowed with an unremitting dread. In an effort to overcome this sensitivity they may, and usually do, resort to malpractices in the hope of establishing an I-don't-care attitude. This course leads down into lower and lower forms of practice until the nervous system is shattered and exhaustion is reached.

There may be glandular abnormalities, or other physical deficiencies upon which any good psychiatrist would look with suspicion. Hence one of the chief departments in the purely physical aspect of the prison environment would be not only an adequate hospitalization, but a super-adequate hospitalization. My own prison hospital experience has convinced me that the physician in charge should be resident; that he should be an able surgeon, physician, and psychiatrist, and a thorough student of the physical causes underlying antisocial behaviour. The prison hospital should be supplied with a staff of experts under such a man, and the aim of prison hospitalization should be to correct abnormal physical conditions and mental and emotional states.

Prison food is one of society's most expensive items. It is behind nearly every prison outbreak, either directly or indirectly. Those who enter prison in good physical health are almost certain to leave it in prison when their terms have been finished. It would be impossible to enumerate the hardened criminals in this country who took their first turn toward bitterness because of prison food. Hence the prison diet is of major importance in building up the physical area of an effective prison system.

Educational opportunities should be studied toward the common end of physical, emotional, and mental correction. Prison recreation should be planned to this same end, as should prison occupation. For if society wants correction in its prisons, then it must discard the old and thoroughly exploded theory of punishment as a deterrent and corrective of criminal tendencies.

Both Father Good and the lifer envisioned a prison system which would meet these basic requirements. Add to this a real and vital prison religion and the prison system would for the first time in civilized history work for and not against the interests of a crime-infected social order.

From these points of view, it is seen that crime is a disease of the conscience. The underlying causes and contributing factors which motivate and progressively establish this disease work through the physical, emotional, and mental organism of the prospective criminal and are supported and encouraged by deficiencies in the early environment.

After the disease has become chronic, no prison system which overemphasizes science and underemphasizes religion can correct the disease, no matter how adequate such a system might be. Science can arrest the progress of a diseased conscience, but it cannot effect a cure. The conscience, being the spiritual area in man's personality, can only respond to spiritual stimuli. Hence the cure for a sick conscience finally waits upon the application of religion. And this religion should appeal to the conscience through inspiration and reason, rather than through fear of divine judgment and eternal condemnation. Such a prison religion would seek to sublimate the energy of sin; it would not use sin as a weapon to coerce the convict into being good. By showing the convict how to reverse the energy of sin, it would give him the incentive and power to effect his own salvation.

What, then, are the requirements of an effective prison system of religion? First of all it would be non-denominational. Second it would develop its own technique for presentation. It would be taken for granted that a minister who had been trained to meet the requirements for a social congregation could not hope to employ the same methods and get outstanding results with an antisocial congregation. There is this unbridgeable difference between the two types of congregations. The members of a social congregation are, as a usual thing, lulled into a false sense of spiritual security. They feel they are saved. So the psychology of such persons becomes extremely simple. The minister needs only a grasp of the scriptures and an ability to verify what his congregation already claims. Generally speaking, he preaches to the "already saved." Whilst on the other hand, the psychology of the convict congregation is just the reverse. There is nothing simple about it. It is, in fact, exceedingly complex. The convict does not embrace any false sense of spiritual security. He lays no claim to being saved. He is a sinner and often takes pride in that fact, and not infrequently, if he is educated, he likes to strut and pose as a brilliant and devastating pagan. But in him there is a lot of sincerity and self-honesty. He is not inclined toward the outside practices of self-deception. And if the inner man of him is understood by the chaplain, his soul can be more readily plucked for Christ than can the soul that slumbers content in its state of prenatal and illusory security. He will pause at no middle ground. He is either against or for Christ. If against him, he is wholly against him. If he is for Christ, he is just as avid in his embracement. He is hot for Christ or coldly against him.

If ministers who have been trained in seminaries are inadequate as prison ministers, what, then, is the answer to this basic problem? From the lifer and Father Good I gathered this answer: A college centrally located for the sole and special training of prison chaplains. It would be an interdenominational college, morally and financially supported by all faiths, as well as by the state and Federal governments, and by all the clubs and societies organized to promote the general welfare.

I hold this to be a vital and far-reaching idea. Therefore, I have included it as an epilogue to this book. It might have been written as an open letter to society and couched in the form of a direct and stirring challenge—for such it is.

Space does not permit me to expand the idea and to show how, step by step, a specially trained prison chaplain would go about his task of healing a diseased conscience. But to any genuine authority, or vitally interested group, I am ever willing and ever ready to render further information, to the extent of my ability.

CPSIA information can be obtained
at www.ICGtesting.com
Printed in the USA
BVHW092327170920
588931BV00009B/626

9 781460 003244